OFFERINGS FROM 'THE OVEN'

by Wendy Louise with MaryAnn Koopmann

A Classic Cookbook with Recipes for Every Occasion

Offerings from the Oven
*A Collection of Recipes
for Every Occasion*

Wendy Louise and MaryAnn Koopmann

Also by Wendy Louise...

The Sensational Skillet Cookbook: Create Spectacular Meals with Your Electric Skillet

The Complete Crockery Cookbook: Create Spectacular Meals with Your Slow Cooker

400 Rush Hour Recipes: Recipes, Tips and Wisdom for Every Day of the Year (co-authored with Brook Noel)

All available at www.championpress.com or wherever books are sold.

CHAMPION PRESS, LTD.
BELGIUM, WISCONSIN
Copyright © 2006 Wendy Louise

All rights reserved. No part of this book shall be reproduced, stored, or transmitted by any means without written permission from the publisher. Although every precaution has been taken in the preparation of this book, the publisher and author assume no responsibility for errors or omissions. Neither is any liability assumed for damages resulting from the use of the information contained herein. For more information contact: Champion Press, Ltd. 765 Main Street, Belgium, WI 53004 or call toll-free 877-250-3354

Reasonable care has been taken in the preparation of the text to insure its clarity and accuracy. The book is sold with the understanding that the author and publisher are not engaged in rendering professional service. The author and publisher specifically disclaim any liability, loss or risk, personal or otherwise, which is incurred as a consequence, directly or indirectly, of the use and application of any of the contents of this book.

ISBN: 1932783911
LCCN: 2004110040

Manufactured in the United States of America

10 9 8 7 6 5 4 3 2 1

For

Dorothy and Dottie
Betty and Peggy
Johanna and Nana
Samantha, Alicia, and Breanne

Contents

(For a complete listing of recipes by type and main ingredient, please see page 345)

9 ... Introduction

11 ... Getting Started

15 ... Chapter One: Starters and Snacks

41 ... Chapter Two: "Pull up a Chair" for Easy and Everyday Fare

69 ... Chapter Three: "Kitchen Klassics" by Classic Cooks

109 ... Chapter Four: "Company's Coming for Dinner; Let's Get Fancy"

161 .,. Chapter Five: The Top Twenty" ... Twenty of Our Favorite Casseroles

189 ... Chapter Six: Seventeen Super "Sides" ... Hot Dishes to Complete Any Meal

213 ... Chapter Seven: "Outside the Oven" ... Adding that Special Touch

255 ... Chapter Eight: "Our Daily Bread"

295 ... Chapter Nine: Sweet Nothings that are Everything—In Other Words, Dessert

345 ... Recipe Index

Introduction

COOKING IS A CRAFT ... an art. Like quilting, scrapbooking, gardening, decorating, sports and hobbies, or even riding a bike ... it takes time, deserves a little practice, and enhances the quality of our lives and the lives of our families and guests.

When we look back through our mother's recipe boxes and scribbled-notes, we discover a journal about our families—a history of tastes and times, evolving over the years. This history evolves around the kitchen table, and for fancier occasions in the dining room. Our mother's scratched-out-recipes, better ones added; coveted recipes from dear friends and inherited ones from generations passed; notes written in the margin, all lovingly adjusted and prepared—to bring health and pleasure and well-being to our families three times a day, every day, every year. Then our additions become added in those margins; the cycle begins again with a new "biography" built in the kitchen and brought to the table.

When MaryAnn's and my mother cooked, there were no convenience-foods, drive-ins, deli-departments, and in-store bakeries. Things were made from scratch—baked in the oven (or cooked on the stove-top), cooled on the counter, and brought to the table in all their delicious splendor for us to enjoy. And it is to these recipes we return today, for nothing beats a good nut bread or a home-baked pie, that special casserole, or just a good oven-baked, butter-basted chicken with mashed potatoes and gravy "just like Mother made."

Un-like our mothers, we don't have to bake and cook from scratch every day—we can add conveniently packaged and prepared ingredients to our recipes; we can easily find ethnic ingredients and 'seasonal' foods that have become available year 'round. When we don't feel like cooking at all, we can enjoy that home-delivered pizza or Chinese take-out that gives us a day off.

But when we want to cook ... we want to cook! And these are the recipes with which to do that. So pull up a chair, make yourself a cup of tea, and enter our kitchens. Within these pages are recipes refined for today's tastes, all palates, and all palettes, by two ordinary people that happen to be extraordinary cooks.

We invite you to pick a recipe and start preheating your oven ...

Wendy Louise and MaryAnn

Getting Started:
A "Baker's Dozen" of Tips

#1- Read your recipe through entirely and make sure you understand its instructions. Check that you have all the ingredients necessary and gather them on your kitchen counter, so you are organized and ready to proceed.

#2- Keep the preheating of your oven to a minimum to reduce energy consumption—about 10 minutes is all that is necessary. Pre-heating your oven is more important for exact-baking, such as breads, popovers, soufflés, and delicate dishes, than when cooking casseroles like lasagna, scalloped potatoes, or vegetables in sauce.

#3- Putting cold or frozen foods in the oven lengthens cooking time. Defrost frozen foods a day ahead of time, or overnight, in the refrigerator. While preheating your oven, pull out refrigerated food and let it start coming to room temperature before you put it in the oven.

#4- Don't over-pack your oven (something we all do during the holidays). Each dish needs circulating air to cook efficiently. You may have to adjust some cooking times.

#5- Get to know your oven—which area cooks faster (the back or perhaps one side) and keep your oven clean (wiping up spills right away, etc.).

#6- Glass (such as Pyrex®) and ceramic casserole dishes cook more efficiently and evenly, and hold their temperature better than inexpensive metal pans. Make sure the dishes you use are 'oven-safe.'

#7- Don't open the oven door any more than necessary, as heat escapes and has to rebuild again every time "you take a peek."

#8- Make a double batch, and freeze one for a future 're-heat' dinner. Just make sure your dish is both oven and freezer proof.

#9- Use a meat thermometer, your oven timer, and doneness-tests (such as toothpick or knife blade inserted in center and coming out clean) so that you don't over-cook your food.

#10-Food still cooks (especially meats) after pulled from the oven and resting before serving. You can loosely "tent' (cover) with foil to keep the foods warm until ready to serve.

#11- Remember heat rises, so cook on center rack when possible. If using both racks in your oven, you might want to stagger foods; change half-way through lower to higher, higher to lower; and rotate back to front, front to back.

#12- When setting your oven, set the temperature for the most important dish (your meat or primary entrée) and pick side-dishes that can be cooked mutually alongside. If you are lucky enough to have two ovens, cook the entrée in one (for example: a turkey or roast) and the side-dishes in the other.

#13- While food is resting, turn off oven, and put in dinner plates to warm. Warm plates are an extra nice touch to complete your lovingly prepared meal. Avoid cold drafts (such as an opened-window) as your food will lose its serving temperature quickly and not be as delicious as you want it to be.

Chapter One
Starters and Snacks

✧

"A smiling face is half the meal."
~Latvian Proverb

Recipe Index

Avocado Puffs ... 17
Marilyn's Crab Quiche with Savory Crumb Crust ... 18
Florida Crackers ... 19
Pearlie Mae's Party Pecans ... 20
Sugar Baked Peanuts ... 20
Prize Potato Chips ... 21
Sammy's Stacker Crackers ... 22
Tomato Pesto Pie ... 23
Bacon Wrapped Bread Sticks ... 24
Bacon Tomato Cups ... 25
Lite Vegetable Pizza ... 26
Sausage Bites ... 27
Stuffed Mushrooms ... 28
Easy Italian Pinwheels ... 29
Bean Dip ... 30
Bernie's Bacon Bites ... 31
Sara's Sassy Spinach Dip ... 32
Olive Shortbread Cookies ... 33

MAK's Potato Nachos ... 34
Oh So Good Chicken Wings ... 35
Spinach-Cheese Squares ... 36
Seafood Puffs ... 37
Chicken Puffs ... 38
Toasted Almond Party Spread ... 40

Avocado Puffs
Makes 24 canapés

Pastry:
Cream Puff Pastry for 24 mini-puffs
 (see page 37 for Cream Puff Pastry directions)

Filling:
1 cup mashed avocado
1 tablespoon lime juice
1 teaspoon salt
Dash of Tabasco
1 clove garlic, smashed and finely minced
1 tablespoon finely grated onion
1/2 teaspoon Worcestershire
6 slices bacon, cooked and crumbled

Place cream puff dough by 1/2 teaspoonfuls on greased cookie sheets. Bake at 425° until firm (about 25 minutes). Cool before filling. Split cooled puffs open and carefully remove any soft dough from centers. Mix filling ingredients together well and divide between puffs. Fill puffs just before serving (or fill slightly ahead of time and store briefly in refrigerator).

A Conversation with the Cook... "This recipe makes a very fancy appetizer that would be wonderful for a special party. You do not want to fill your puffs too far in advance at the risk of them getting soggy."

Marilyn's Crab Quiche with Savory Crumb Crust

Makes 1 pie

Crust:
1 cup cornflakes, crushed fine in a blender
1/2 stick butter, melted
1/2 teaspoon crushed tarragon

Filling:
1 cup cream-style cottage cheese
3 egg yolks
1/2 cup half-and-half cream
3 tablespoons flour
1/2 teaspoon salt
1/8 teaspoon pepper
1 tablespoon chopped chives or green onion tops
1 tablespoon lemon juice
6 ounces king crab meat
3 egg whites, beaten stiff

Make crust by blending together cereal crumbs, melted butter, and tarragon. Press into bottom and sides of pie pan; set aside. Put first 8 filling ingredients in blender and blend until smooth. Add crab meat; blend to mix; set aside. Beat egg whites stiff. Gently fold contents of blender into egg whites and pour filling into crust. Bake at 350° for 30 to 35 minutes, or until knife pierced in center comes out clean. Serve hot, cut into small wedges, as a first course or appetizer. ~*recipe courtesy of Nancy, in honor of her sister Marilyn*

A Conversation with the Cook... "Elegant and rich, but light and delicate, Marilyn's quiche makes an impressive first course."

✧

Florida Crackers
Makes 30 crackers

15 bacon slices, halved, cooked until limp, and drained on paper toweling
10 rectangular crackers (preferably Waverly®) broken into thirds along their perforations
Parmesan cheese
Fresh apple slices

Wrap a limp bacon-half around each cracker-third. Place seam-side-down on a broiler rack. Sprinkle with Parmesan cheese. Bake at 350° for 10 minutes, or until crisp. Serve with slices of fresh apple.

A Conversation with the Cook... "This recipe comes from a Floridian who used to entertain with great flair. The crispness of the apple slices adds that extra touch that completes the dish."

Pearlie Mae's Party Pecans
Makes 1 cup

1 cup pecans
1 tablespoon olive oil
1 tablespoon Worcestershire
Salt

Mix nuts with olive oil and Worcestershire to coat. Spread on cookie sheet. Bake at 275° for 30 minutes, stirring often. Drain on paper toweling and sprinkle with a little salt while still warm.

A Conversation with the Cook... "Both of these recipes are great as a light munchie to serve with a chilled aperitif before dinner."

Sugar Baked Peanuts
Makes 6 cups

6 cups peanuts, unsalted with skins
2 cups sugar
1 cup water

Place peanuts with sugar and water in a large skillet. Stir constantly, over high-heat on stove-top, until water evaporates and crystals form on nuts. Pour onto foil-lined baking sheets. Bake at 300° for 1 hour, shaking occasionally. Cool and store indefinitely in tightly-lidded Mason® jars.

Prize Potato Chips
Novelty recipe

2 or 3 baking potatoes, scrubbed and cleaned
Melted butter
Fresh parsley leaves
Parchment paper
2 cookie sheets and a weight (for pressing down the top cookie sheet)

Make the thinnest possible potato slices. (You can leave the skins on or off—your choice.) To assemble: Line your bottom cookie sheet with a piece of parchment paper. Paint the paper with melted butter. Lay on a single layer of potato slices. Spread slices with melted butter and place a parsley leaf (or two) on the center of each chip. In "sandwich" fashion, place another potato slice on top of each parsley-ed slice. When finished, cover all with a second piece of buttered parchment paper. Top with second cookie sheet. Weight down the top cookie sheet to flatten all. (An old fashioned cast iron skillet makes a perfect weight.) Put entire assemblage in oven and bake at 400° for 6 minutes. Rotate pan and bake 6 minutes more, for a total of 12 minutes. Serve freshly made.

A Conversation with the Cook... "A tad labor intensive, but fun to make. For ease of slicing, use a very sharp knife or a fancy gadget called a Mandolin, if you have it. Serve as a light appetizer or as a special plate-garnish with grilled steaks."

Sammy's Stacker Crackers
A kid friendly recipe

1 box Wasa® crackers, original flavor
Olive oil
Shredded mozzarella cheese
Italian seasoning

Place a cracker on a microwave safe dish. Spread a thin layer of olive oil. Sprinkle on cheese. Top with a pinch of seasoning. Heat in microwave until cheese begins to melt. Eat while warm. These make a easy snack or appetizer. Change it up with pizza sauce in place of olive oil for a pizza-taste.

A Conversation with the Cook... "Whenever I have friends over after school, I show them how to make this snack. Everyone loves it!"

"Food is an important part of a balanced diet."
~Anonymous

Tomato Pesto Pie
Makes 6 to 8 servings

1/2 cup of your favorite pesto
1 (12-inch) pizza crust, pre-baked according to package instructions
3 to 4 sun-ripened garden tomatoes, seeded and sliced
Freshly cracked pepper to taste
1/2 cup drained and sliced, pitted black olives
A slight drizzle of Balsamic vinegar
2 cups shredded mozzarella cheese

Pre-bake the pizza crust; set aside. Spread pesto sauce evenly over crust. Slice tomatoes thin and arrange on top of pesto. Freshly crack pepper over all. Sprinkle on olives. Drizzle with a few drops of Balsamic vinegar. Sprinkle on cheese. Bake in 425° oven until cheese melts and tomatoes are warmed through. Cut into appetizer-size wedges.

A Conversation with the Cook... "To seed tomatoes, cut in half and gently squeeze the extra juice and seeds out of each half. Proceed to slice and use in your recipe. For easy slicing, always use a very sharp, and even serrated, knife to cut your tomatoes.

Bacon Wrapped Bread Sticks

Makes 6 to 8 servings

1 package, plain flavored Italian bread sticks (found in the specialty cracker section of your market)
1 pound bacon
Parmesan cheese, divided

Cut each bacon slice down the middle lengthwise, to make 2 long strips per slice. Wrap 1 thin bacon strip, spiraling around (diagonally) on each breadstick. Roll in Parmesan cheese, coating well. Put a cake-cooling rack in a large pan with sides. (I like to use a jelly roll pan.) Place prepared bread sticks on rack. Bake at 350° until bacon is done. Take out of oven and re-roll baked sticks in additional Parmesan cheese while sticks are still hot. Serve warm for best flavor.

A Conversation with the Cook... "These are so easy and make an impressive finger-food for family gatherings and parties. For easy clean up, put foil under the rack to catch any spills."

Bacon Tomato Cups

Makes 12 servings

8 slices bacon, fried crisp and crumbled
1 medium tomato, seeded and chopped
1 small onion, chopped fine
3 ounces Swiss cheese, shredded
1/2 cup Miracle Whip®
1 1/2 teaspoons dried basil
1 (10 ounce) tube flaky biscuits

Mix bacon, tomato, onion, cheese, Miracle Whip®, and basil together. Split each biscuit into halves and press into muffin tins. Fill with mixture. Bake at 375° for 10 to 12 minutes until golden brown. Serve warm.

A Conversation with the Cook... "These can be made ahead of time and freeze very well. They are great to have on hand for unexpected guests or during the holidays, when you need a last minute appetizer. Just reheat in the microwave or warm in the oven."

Lite Vegetable Pizza

Makes 12 servings

2 (10 ounce) tubes low-fat crescent-style rolls
12 ounces non-fat soft cream cheese
3/4 cup non-fat Kraft® Peppercorn Ranch Dressing
1 1/2 tablespoons Accent® seasoning
1 tablespoon parsley flakes
1 tablespoon dill weed
1 tablespoon minced onion
1 teaspoon seasoned salt
1 cup broccoli
1 cup cauliflower
1/2 cup mushrooms
1/2 cup black olives
1/2 cup tomatoes

Spread and pat crescent rolls on a cookie sheet to make a "pizza" crust. Bake at 375° for 10 minutes. Cool. Meanwhile mix cream cheese, dressing, Accent®, parsley flakes, dill weed, onion, and salt. Spread mixture over cooled crust. Top with raw vegetables. Cut into squares to serve.

A Conversation with the Cook... "Best if eaten right away but you can keep covered in refrigerator, to keep fresh for leftovers. With all its non-fat and low-fat ingredients you don't have to feel guilty about sneaking out to the fridge for a 'midnight-snack.'"

Sausage Bites
Makes 3 dozen

1 pound bulk pork sausage
1 beaten egg
1/2 cup fine dry bread crumbs
1/3 cup milk
1/3 teaspoon sage
1/2 cup water
1/4 cup catsup
2 tablespoons brown sugar, packed
1 tablespoon vinegar
1 tablespoon soy sauce
Rye crackers, at serving time

Combine sausage, egg, bread crumbs, milk, and sage. Beat at high speed for 5 minutes. Shape mixture into 3 dozen 1-inch balls. Brown on cookie sheet in 325° oven for 25 minutes. Meanwhile simmer water, catsup, brown sugar, vinegar, and soy sauce to make a marinade. Remove sausage balls from oven and place in serving dish. Pour marinade-sauce over sausage balls and toss all to coat. Serve warm and accompany with rye crackers.

A Conversation with the Cook... "Make this a day ahead and let sausage balls marinate in sauce for extra flavor and convenience. Reheat to serve."

Stuffed Mushrooms
Makes approximately 12 servings

1 pound whole fresh mushrooms, select mushrooms with choice, firm caps
1 pound ground beef
1 envelope dry onion soup mix
8 ounces Cheddar cheese, grated
1/8 teaspoon black pepper

Clean mushrooms and remove stems from caps. Set caps aside and chop stems. Brown ground beef, soup mix, black pepper, and mushroom stems together to make a filling. Remove from heat and stir in cheese. Let filling cool. Stuff mushroom caps with cooled filling and bake for 10 to 15 minutes at 350°. Serve warm.

A Conversation with the Cook... "When buying mushrooms, caps should be closed around the stems, tight and firm. Avoid exposed black or brown gills, or discoloring caps, as this means the mushrooms are no longer fresh. Clean mushrooms by brushing with a soft brush. Since mushrooms are comprised mostly of water, you do not want to clean them by washing—as they will soften and turn slimy when stored, or will steam instead of sauté when cooked."

Easy Italian Pinwheels
Makes 2 dozen

1/2 cup mozzarella cheese
1/2 cup sliced pepperoni, finely chopped
1/2 teaspoon crushed oregano leaves
1 egg yolk
1 (8 ounce) can Pillsbury® Refrigerated Quick Crescent Dinner Rolls
1 egg white, beaten

In small bowl, combine cheese, pepperoni, oregano, and egg yolk, mixing well. Separate dough into 4 rectangles. Firmly press perforation to seal. Spread each rectangle with about 3 tablespoons meat mixture. Starting at the shortest end, roll up each rectangle, pinching edges to seal. Cut each roll into 6 slices. Place cut-side-down and 1-inch apart on un-greased cookie sheet. Brush with beaten egg white. Bake at 375° for 12 to 15 minutes or until golden brown. Serve these pretty pinwheels warm.

A Conversation with the Cook... "To make ahead, assemble, cover with plastic wrap, and refrigerate up to 2 hours before baking. Bake as directed above at time of serving."

Bean Dip
Makes 12 servings

1 (15 ounce) can refried beans
16 ounces soft cream cheese
16 ounces sour cream
1 small package taco seasoning mix
8 ounces Monterey Jack cheese, shredded
8 ounces Cheddar cheese, shredded
Taco chips, at serving time

Combine first four ingredients and place in a non-stick sprayed heat-proof baking dish. Bake at 350° for 20 minutes. Top with shredded cheeses, and serve warm with chips for dipping.

A Conversation with the Cook... "A great dip for teens, my son always asked for this one when he had friends over. For an extra treat, serve multi-colored corn chips for an authentic south-of-the border taste."

"Let my words, like vegetables, be tender and sweet,
for tomorrow I may have to eat them."
~Unknown

Bernie's Bacon Bites
Makes several dozen for a party or special gathering

1 (10.5 ounce) can cream of mushroom soup
Soft white bread slices, crusts removed (use soft white bread such as Bunny® or Wonder® bread)
1 pound package standard-cut bacon
Toothpicks (optional)

Cut crusts off of bread slices and spread each slice with cream of mushroom soup, straight from the can. Roll up jelly-roll fashion. Wrap each roll diagonally with a slice of bacon. Cut into thirds and secure with toothpicks if desired (each roll will yield 3 bacon bites). Arrange on non-stick-sprayed cookie sheet in single layer. Bake at 350° for 30 minutes. Drain on paper toweling and serve warm, from a napkin-lined basket.

A Conversation with the Cook... "How can something so simple as Bernie's recipe ... be so good?"

✧

Sara's Sassy Spinach Dip
Makes enough for a party or special gathering

1 stick butter
1 tablespoon minced garlic clove
1 medium onion, diced
2 (10 ounce) packages frozen spinach, thawed and

well drained
1 (14 ounce) can artichoke hearts, drained and cut into quarters
1 (8 ounce) package cream cheese (fat-free will NOT work)
1 (8 ounce) package sour cream (again fat-free is NOT an option; this isn't a dip for those on a diet)
1 cup freshly grated Parmesan cheese (grate fresh from a wedge of cheese)
1 cup Italian-blend cheese (Asiago, Romano, and Mozzarella)
1 1/2 tablespoons hot sauce
Rye or tortilla chips, at time of serving
Fresh vegetable crudités (optional), at time of serving

Melt butter in skillet over medium heat. Add onion and garlic and sauté until soft but not browned (approximately 5 minutes). Stir in remaining ingredients (except chips) until well blended. Transfer warm mixture to buttered, medium-size, oven-proof casserole dish and bake at 350° for 12 minutes. Serve warm with chips or fresh vegetables for dipping.

A Conversation with the Cook... "This very rich dip has become a 'must' for parties and especially our holiday gatherings. We like to use those little 'cup-shaped' tortilla chips for dipping, so we get a lot of dip with each bite!"

"Cooking is a craft—an art. It takes time, deserves a little practice, and enhances the quality of our lives and the lives of our guests." ~Wendy Louise

Olive Shortbread Cookies

Makes 24 appetizer cookies

6 tablespoons butter, softened
1 1/3 cups grated Cheddar cheese
1 1/2 teaspoons parsley flakes (or use finely minced fresh)
1/8 teaspoon onion powder
Dash cayenne
2/3 cups flour
24 pimento-stuffed green olives

Cream butter and Cheddar cheese until smooth. Blend in seasonings. Gradually mix in flour until all is blended and smooth. Drop by teaspoonfuls onto ungreased cookie sheet. Firmly place an olive in center of each cookie. Bake at 400° for 15 to 20 minutes. Serve warm.

A Conversation with the Cook... "These appetizer cookies just melt in your mouth."

MAK's Potato Nachos
Makes 12 servings

6 medium potatoes, thinly sliced
1 (8 ounce) jar Mexican Cheez Whiz®
Salt and pepper to taste
1 bunch green onions, chopped
2 medium tomatoes, seeded and chopped
1 (4 ounce) container sour cream

Spread potato slices on greased cookie sheets. Salt and pepper to taste. Bake in 375° oven for 25 to 30 minutes. Place on serving dish. Heat processed cheese, according to label's directions; pour over potatoes. Top with green onions, tomatoes, and sour cream.

A Conversation with the Cook... "Get out your football schedule and serve this at your next game-party."

Oh So Good Chicken Wings
Never makes enough; you can't stop eating 'em

4 pounds chicken wings
1 cup butter
2 1/4 cups grated Parmesan cheese
4 tablespoons chopped parsley
1 teaspoon salt
2 tablespoons crushed oregano
4 teaspoons paprika
1 teaspoon pepper

Cut tips from wings and discard. Cut trimmed wings in half at the joint, making 2 pieces per wing. Melt butter and set aside. Mix remaining ingredients together, to form a dipping-coating. Dip wings in butter, then in cheese mixture to coat. Arrange in shallow foil-lined baking dish. Drizzle with any remaining butter and bake at 350° for 1 hour. Serve warm.

A Conversation with the Cook... "These can be made ahead and reheated. They also can be frozen (before being cooked) and baked later. So for a future date go ahead and double your batch. Just remember, if pulling from the freezer to add a few extra minutes to your cooking time. These may be served as is, or with a dipping sauce of Blue Cheese Dressing or Ranch Dressing for dipping. A nice addition would be our Mayonnaise Frenchaise (see page 216 for recipe)."

Spinach-Cheese Squares
Makes 12 servings

4 tablespoons butter
3 eggs
1 cup flour
1 cup milk
1/2 teaspoon salt
1 teaspoon baking soda
1 pound Cheddar cheese, grated
2 box-packages chopped spinach, thawed and drained well

Preheat oven to 350°. In a 13 x 9-inch pan, melt the butter in oven; remove pan from oven. In bowl, beat eggs. Add flour, milk, salt, and baking powder, mixing well. Add cheese and spinach and blend. Pour mixture into buttered pan and return pan to oven to bake at 350° for 35 minutes to set. Cut into bite size squares and serve warm or at room temperature.

A Conversation with the Cook... "Can freeze by placing squares on cookie sheet; freeze solid. Place in plastic bags and store. To serve, re-heat 12 minutes at 325°. For a more diet-conscious variation you can use cooking spray instead of the 4 tablespoons of butter to grease your pan."

"I'm strong to the finich, 'cause I eats my spinach, I'm Popeye the sailorman."
~song lyrics from "Popeye the Sailor Man," by Sammy Lerner, 1933

Seafood Puffs

Makes 12 servings

Pastry for Puffs:
1 cup sifted flour
1/2 teaspoon salt
1 cup water
1/2 cup butter
4 eggs

Mix flour and salt and set aside. Heat water and butter in saucepan until butter melts. Add flour all at once and beat vigorously over low heat until mixture leaves sides of pan and begins to form a ball. Cool slightly. Add unbeaten eggs, one at a time, beating thoroughly after each addition. Drop small teaspoonfuls on greased baking sheets about 1-inch apart. Bake at 400° for 15 to 25 minutes, watching carefully not to burn. Split when cool and fill with seafood filling. Continue with recipe as written below.

Seafood Filling:
1 package frozen crabmeat, thawed
1 can bay shrimp, drained
1 cup mushroom soup, undiluted
1/4 cup green pepper, minced
1 tiny jar pimiento, chopped
1/4 teaspoon salt
Dash of cayenne pepper
3 tablespoons Sherry
1 cup buttered bread crumbs

Combine all ingredients to make a filling. Fill puffs and place on cookie sheets. Bake at 350° for 8 to 10 minutes.

A Conversation with the Cook... "When I want an extravagant appetizer either one of my Puff Recipes is it."

✧

Chicken Puffs
Makes 12 servings

For Puffs:
2 tablespoons butter
1/4 cup boiling water
1/4 cup flour
Dash of salt
1 egg
1/4 pound Swiss cheese, shredded

For Filling:
2 cups chopped cooked chicken, or canned chicken
1/4 cup celery, finely chopped
1/4 cup mayonnaise
1/2 teaspoon additional salt
Dash of pepper

Melt butter in 1/4 cup boiling water. Add flour and dash of salt; stir vigorously. Cook and stir until mixture forms a ball that doesn't separate. Remove from heat and cool slightly. Add egg and beat vigorously till smooth. Stir in cheese. Drop dough on un-greased baking sheet, using 1 level teaspoon of dough for each puff. Bake at 400° for about 20 minutes. Remove puffs from oven. Cool and split. Combine remaining ingredients to make a filling. Fill each puff with 2 teaspoons filling and serve.

A Conversation with the Cook... "If you have leftover chicken make these melt-in-your mouth appetizers the next day."

Toasted Almond Party Spread

Makes 12 servings

1 (6 ounce) package cream cheese
1 1/2 cups Swiss cheese, shredded
1/2 cup Miracle Whip®
1 green onion, chopped with green top
1/8 teaspoon ground nutmeg
1/8 teaspoon pepper
1/3 cup toasted almonds
Good crackers, at serving time

Combine all ingredients (except toasted almonds); spread in 9-inch pie pan, or similar dish. Bake 15 to 20 minutes (depending on desired brownness on top). Stir halfway through baking (at 8 to 12 minutes). Top with toasted almonds. Serve with crackers.

A Conversation with the Cook... "There are 3 ways to toast nuts:

(1) Stir in a dry skillet over medium heat until golden brown (2) spread on a cookie sheet and bake in moderate oven until golden brown (3) put under broiler until fully toasted. Whichever you pick, keep an eye on them, because almonds will toast very quickly, and you definitely don't want to burn them!"

Chapter Two
"Pull up a chair" for Easy and Everyday Fare

✧

"Kissing don't last; cookery do."
~George Merideth, as wise man

Recipe Index

Cheese Strata with Corn Flake Topping ... 43
The King's Chicken ... 44
Audra's Chicken and Rice Casserole ... 45
Mom's Pork Chop Casserole ... 47
Ham and Broccoli Roll-ups ... 48
Too Easy Pot Roast ... 49
Peggy's Potato Pie ... 50
Dad's BBQ Baby Back Ribs ... 51
Glenn's Pizza Noodle Hot Dish ... 52
Family Favorite Beef Taco Bake ... 53
MaryAnn's Golden Fish Puffs ... 54
Chicken Breasts with Cheese and Tomato ... 55
Angie's Italian Beef ... 56
Glenn's Oven Baked Pork ... 57
Hunter's Delight ... 58
Liver Spanish Style ... 59
Oven Stew ... 60
Angie's Super Supper Roast ... 61

Alicia's Baked Chop Suey ... 62
MaryAnn's Magic Turkey Loaf ... 63
Chicken Enchiladas ... 64
Impossible Taco Pie ... 66
Poppy Seed Chicken ... 67
Glenn's Salmon Casserole ... 68

Cheese Strata with Corn Flake Topping

Makes 6 to 6+ servings

6 slices bread, buttered and cubed
1 1/2 cups shredded Cheddar cheese, divided
3 to 4 eggs (depending on size of eggs used)
1 1/2 to 2 cups milk
1/2 to 1 teaspoon dry mustard
1/2 teaspoon salt
Dash cayenne
1 tablespoon Worcestershire
Crushed cornflakes and dots of butter, to make a topping

Place half of buttered bread cubes in buttered casserole or soufflé dish, or a 9 x 13-inch buttered baking dish. Sprinkle on half of cheese. Place on remaining half of bread cubes. Top with remaining half of cheese. Beat together next 6 ingredients and pour over all. Cover and let stand all day or overnight in fridge. When ready to bake, sprinkle with crushed corn flakes and dot with butter for a topping. Bake at 325° for 50 to 55 minutes, till set. You can check for doneness by inserting the blade of a knife in the center, if blade comes out clean, it's done. If not—cook the strata for a few more minutes. Let stand 10 minutes before serving.

A Conversation with the Cook... "This is a dish that has the great convenience of being assembled ahead of time and fits nicely into a busy schedule, served as breakfast, brunch, lunch or dinner!"

The King's Chicken
Makes 4 to 6 servings

1 (3 to 4 pound) plump, whole chicken
Seasonings of salt, pepper, and sweet paprika
Melted butter
Lemon juice, optional

Remove any giblets (and save for gravy if you wish) from cavity of chicken. Rinse chicken and pat dry. Season inside-and-out with salt, pepper, and paprika for color. Bake, un-stuffed, for 1 1/2 hours at 400°, or until juices from chicken run clear. Baste often with melted butter while cooking. When done, remove to platter and drizzle pan juices over chicken or make gravy if you wish. A nice touch, but not necessary, is to squeeze some fresh lemon juice over the chicken, before carving.

A Conversation with the Cook... "Yes, before KFC™, there was such a thing as delicious chicken, without all the bells and whistles, dips and batters! Make this dinner on a cozy winter night, and return your family to 'real chicken ... cooked in a real kitchen ... by a real cook' ... they just might be delightfully surprised."

"No peasant in my kingdom shall lack the means to have a chicken in the pot every Sunday."
~Henry IV, King of France

Audra's Chicken and Rice Casserole

Makes 4 to 6 servings

1 (10 ounce) package frozen broccoli spears (chopped)
1 cup grated Velveeta® cheese, divided
2 cups cubed cooked chicken
Salt and pepper to taste
1 cup cooked rice (white, brown, or wild rice)
2 tablespoons butter
2 tablespoons flour
1 cup milk
1 tablespoon lemon juice
1 cup sour cream

Cook broccoli according to package directions; drain well and chop. Arrange chopped broccoli in non-stick sprayed 13 x 9-inch baking dish. Sprinkle with half the cheese. Top with cubed chicken. Season with salt and pepper to taste. Spoon on cooked rice. In a saucepan melt butter over low heat; blend in flour, then milk. Cook stirring constantly till sauce bubbles and thickens. Remove from heat; stir in lemon juice; fold in sour cream. Spread over chicken-rice mixture in casserole dish. Sprinkle with remaining half of cheese. Bake at 400° for 15 to 20 minutes, or until all is heated through and sauce is bubbly. *~recipe courtesy of Audra Le Normand, Liberty Texas*

A Conversation with the Cook... "Rather than buying chopped broccoli, buy the stalk and florets—so you can chop them yourself, for a 'rustic' cut. For variations of this casserole, try any of your choice of the mixed vegetables, found in the freezer department of your market (such as a broccoli-cauliflower-carrot-mix; or mixed stir-fry vegetables. If you prefer green beans to broccoli—that would be good too!"

Mom's Pork Chop Casserole

Makes 6 servings, at 1 chop per person

6 bone-in pork chops (I like to use a "family pack" for this)
Baking potatoes, washed and peeled
Flour
Butter
Milk
Crushed oregano

Slice potatoes thin and arrange in a 9 x 13-inch (buttered) Pyrex® baking dish. Keep slicing in potatoes until you make a layer at least 1-inch deep. Dot the potato layer with butter and sprinkle with a little flour. Lay the pork chops on top of the potato layer. Pour milk over all, until it is about 1/2-inch deep, up the sides of the dish. Sprinkle crushed oregano over the chops. Bake at 350° for 1 1/2 hours. Potatoes should be bubbling and fork-tender, and chops nicely browned when casserole is done.

A Conversation with the Cook... "This dish takes me back to my childhood ... the aroma of this casserole filtering from my mother's kitchen ... hmm, hmm, hmm! When dinnertime was announced, I was the first one to 'pull up a chair' at the table!"

Ham and Broccoli Roll-Ups

Makes 4 to 6 servings

6 spears of fresh broccoli, par-boiled to almost tender
6 slices of ham from the deli
6 slices of Swiss cheese

White Sauce:
1 tablespoon margarine or butter
2 tablespoons flour
2 teaspoons dry mustard
1 1/2 cups milk, added slowly
Salt, pepper, and paprika to taste

Topping:
Parmesan cheese
Dots of butter

Lay out each ham slice; cover each with a piece of Swiss cheese, then place a cooked broccoli spear at one end. Roll up jelly roll fashion (broccoli will be in center, ham on the outside). Arrange rolls side-by-side in single layer in a buttered baking dish. Set aside. In a saucepan, over medium heat, make a sauce starting with a roux of the butter and flour. Once combined stir in dry mustard. Keep whisking and slowly stir in milk to arrive at a fairly thick, smooth white sauce. Season to taste with salt, pepper, and paprika. Pour completed sauce over roll-ups in baking dish. Sprinkle casserole with grated Parmesan and dot with butter. Bake at 450° until thoroughly heated through, a little browned on top, and bubbly.

A Conversation with the Cook... "These Roll-Ups cook up much fancier than the ingredients first appear. They'll think you 'slaved all day' over this one—a great recipe for the beginner cook."

✧

Too Easy Pot Roast
Makes 6 servings

1 (4 pound) chuck roast
1 packet Lipton® Onion Soup Mix

Sprinkle both sides of roast with onion soup mix. Wrap the roast in a double layer of aluminum foil, making a neatly sealed package. Lay package in a baking pan. Place in oven and bake for 4 hours at 325°. Unwrap, slice, and serve. Add sides of parsley-boiled new potatoes or buttered noodles.

A Conversation with the Cook... "This is so easy, fool proof, and delicious it doesn't even need a recipe! Pop it in the oven; go off to see a matinee movie; and when you return, dinner is ready. This is a perfect recipe for the beginner cook or a busy bachelor."

"In cooking, as in the arts,
simplicity is a sign of perfection."
~Curnonsky

Peggy's Potato Pie
Makes 6 to 8 servings

1 (9-inch) deep-dish pie shell, pre-baked and cooled
2 to 2 1/2 cups left-over mashed potatoes (or can use instant potatoes)
3 tablespoons melted butter
1/2 teaspoon salt
1/2 teaspoon white pepper
1/2 cup sour cream
1 cup shredded sharp Cheddar cheese
2 tomatoes, seeded and sliced thin
A drizzle of Balsamic vinegar
1 tablespoon additional butter
1 to 2 tablespoons grated Parmesan cheese
Sour cream for garnish
Freshly chopped chives, for garnish

Bake a single pie crust according to package directions; set aside. While crust is cooling, in a mixer combine mashed potatoes with next 4 ingredients listed, blending until smooth; set aside. Arrange the Cheddar cheese in a layer over the pie crust. Spoon potato mixture on top of cheese layer in pie shell. Arrange tomato slices on top of potato layer, just around the outer edge of pie, overlapping as need be to form an outer ring. Drizzle tomatoes only, with a few drops of Balsamic vinegar. Dot both exposed potatoes and tomatoes with butter. Sprinkle with grated Parmesan. Bake at 400° for 20 to 30 minutes, or until thoroughly heated through and topping is golden brown. Garnish each serving with a dollop of sour cream and a sprinkling of fresh chives. Serve warm as a light entrée or a hearty side dish.

A Conversation with the Cook... "For a creamier version of Peggy's pie, replace the shredded Cheddar with shredded Swiss, Mozzarella, or Gruyere. For a fancier version use the Gruyere cheese; cut pie into slimmer wedges to serve as a first course; and top the sour cream garnish with a little mound of caviar to replace the chives. Peggy's Pie would make a nice accompaniment to Dad's BBQ Baby Back Ribs (see recipe that follows."

Dad's BBQ Baby Back Ribs

Makes 4 servings, at 1/2 rack per person

2 racks of baby back spare ribs, each rack cut in half
Open Pit® barbecue sauce (original flavor)

Roast un-adorned ribs in a hot oven at 450° for 30 minutes to start releasing fat. Reduce heat to 325° and continue to bake 1 1/2 hours more. Last hour of baking start basting frequently with Open Pit® barbecue sauce, to glaze the ribs nicely.

A Conversation with the Cook... "Place ribs bone-side down, meaty side arching-up, so fats will drain off meat and into bottom of pan. Use a disposable foil pan for easy clean-up or line a pan with heavy-duty foil."

Glenn's Pizza Noodle Hot Dish
Makes 6 servings

1 pound ground beef
3 cups noodles, cooked and drained according to package directions
3 cups tomato sauce
1/2 cup green pepper, chopped
1/2 cup onion, chopped
1/2 teaspoon garlic powder
1/2 teaspoon oregano
1/2 teaspoon onion salt
1/2 teaspoon black pepper
4 ounces Parmesan cheese, grated
1 (4 ounce) can mushroom pieces, drained

Sauté ground beef in nonstick skillet; add green pepper and onions and continue to sauté to soften. Meanwhile blend garlic, oregano, onion salt, and black pepper into the tomato sauce and add sauce to skillet. Simmer this mixture for 15 minutes to blend flavors. Meanwhile cook noodles, drain, and place in bottom of non-stick sprayed 13 x 9-inch nonstick baking pan. Pour skillet mixture evenly over noodles. Sprinkle cheese evenly on top and arrange mushrooms over all. Bake, covered with foil, at 350° for 25 minutes. Cool slightly before cutting into squares.

A Conversation with the Cook... "Always let a baked dish 'set up' for 5 or 10 minutes before cutting. This makes portions easier to cut and more attractive to serve."

Family-Favorite Beef Taco Bake
Makes 6 servings

1 pound lean ground beef
1 (10.75 ounce) can tomato soup
1 cup thick and chunky salsa
1/2 cup milk
6 (8-inch) flour tortillas, cut into wedges
1 cup shredded Cheddar cheese, divided
1 (4 ounce) carton sour cream, at serving time

In medium-size skillet over medium-high heat, cook ground beef until browned, stirring to separate meat. Pour off any excess fat. Add soup, salsa, milk, tortillas, and half the cheese. Spoon into 2-quart shallow baking dish. Cover. Bake at 400° for 30 minutes or until hot. Sprinkle with remaining cheese. Top with dabs of sour cream on each serving.

A Conversation with the Cook... "Add green peppers and onions (to taste) to the casserole for variation of flavor. Always select a lean ground beef and drain off any extra fats to minimize fat-content of dish."

MaryAnn's Golden Fish Puffs
Makes 4 servings

1 (16 ounce) package frozen Pike fillets, thawed
Salt, to taste
Pepper, to taste
1 egg white
1/4 teaspoon additional salt
1/4 cup mayonnaise
1/4 teaspoon dill seed
1/4 teaspoon onion juice
Lemon wedges, at serving time
Your favorite tartar sauce, at serving time

Season fish fillets with salt and pepper to taste and place in greased 11 1/2 x 7 1/2 x 1 1/2-inch baking dish. Beat egg white with 1/4 teaspoon salt until stiff but not dry. Fold in remaining ingredients; spoon the batter over fish. Bake uncovered at 425° for 12 to 15 minutes, or until fish flakes easily when cut with fork and topping is puffed and brown. Serve with lemon wedges and your favorite tartar sauce on the side (or see page 218 for homemade tartar sauce recipe).

A Conversation with the Cook... "If you don't have a fisherman in the family, store-bought Pike, Perch, Sole, Pollock, and/or Halibut can all be used in this recipe. Buy fresh fillets from the counter, held on ice; or use good quality flash-frozen from the freezer department."

Chicken Breasts with Cheese and Tomato

Makes 8 servings

8 boned and skinned chicken breast halves
8 slices Swiss or American cheese
1 (10.75ounce) can cream of chicken soup, stirred
8 thin tomato slices
2 tablespoons butter
1/2 cup stuffing-croutons, crushed
Noodles or rice, at serving time

In a 3-quart, oblong baking dish, place chicken breast halves. Top each breast with 1 slice of cheese. Stir soup and spread over cheese. Top each breast with 1 slice of tomato. Combine melted butter with the crushed stuffing; put a spoonful on each tomato. Place baking dish in a 400° oven and bake for 30 minutes, or until juices from chicken run clear. Prepare noodles or rice, and serve on the side.

A Conversation with the Cook... "My family loves this dish, but it is also a great company pleaser—easy to make, and easy to serve."

Angie's Italian Beef

Makes 6 servings

1 (3 to 4 pound) sirloin tip roast
2 cups water
5 beef bouillon cubes
1 teaspoon dried oregano
2 teaspoons dried basil
1/2 teaspoon crushed red pepper
1/2 teaspoon garlic powder
1 teaspoon celery salt
1/8 teaspoon pepper
1 package dry onion soup mix
Good rolls, at serving time or mashed potatoes

Mix all dry ingredients together to make a "rub." Pat rub on top of roast. Place roast in pan and pour water, along with the bouillon cubes, around the sides. Be careful not to pour water over roast—you don't want to disturb the rub. Cover and bake 325° for 30 minutes per pound. Let cool. Slice thin—return meat to liquid and simmer. Serve with good rolls, to make hot beef sandwiches or serve with mashed potatoes on the side.

A Conversation with the Cook... "This dish fills the kitchen with inviting aromas while cooking. You'll hardly be able to wait to get to the table."

Glenn's Oven-Baked Pork
Makes 6 to 8 servings

8 (bone in) pork steaks, chops, or ribs
1 cup catsup
2 tablespoons brown sugar
4 tablespoons lemon juice
3 tablespoons Worcestershire sauce
1/2 tablespoon ground (dry) mustard
1/4 teaspoon thyme
Salt and pepper, at the table

Put meat in pan. (Do not salt and pepper meat at this time.) Mix remaining ingredients and pour over meat. Cover with foil. Bake at 350° for 2 1/2 hours. Let everyone salt and pepper their own portions when served.

A Conversation with the Cook... "Meat with the bone-in will cook faster than a boneless chop. The bone carries the heat to the inside more quickly and also makes for a tastier cut of meat. So this is one recipe where the bones add extra flavor to the meal."

Hunter's Delight

Makes 6 servings

1 pound ground beef
1 (15 ounce) can tomato sauce
1 teaspoon salt
1 teaspoon pepper
1 teaspoon garlic salt
1 medium onion
1 1/2 small packages cream cheese, softened
1 (8 ounce) carton sour cream
1 (8 ounce) package noodles, cooked
Grated cheese

Brown the ground beef; drain. Add tomato sauce and seasonings; mix well. Combine onion, cream cheese, and sour cream, mixing well. Layer the noodles, then beef mixture, then sour cream mixture into a lightly greased baking dish. Top with grated cheese. Bake at 350° for 35 minutes.

A Conversation with the Cook... "My husband is crazy about this casserole; it's easy and simple but so tasty."

Liver Spanish Style
Makes 4 servings

1 large onion, sliced and divided
1 container liver, use very fresh, select pieces
1/2 cup flour
1 (15 ounce) can tomatoes
2 small green peppers, ribbed, seeded, and chopped fine
Salt
Pepper
1 pound bacon
Boiling water

Place in a baking dish a layer of sliced onion, then slices of liver that have been cut thin and rolled in flour. On the liver place another layer of onions, then tomatoes, then green peppers, chopped fine. Salt and pepper to taste. Cover with a layer of sliced bacon. Pour enough boiling water over all so as not to scorch while baking. Bake at 350° for 1 1/2 to 2 hours in the oven, adding water as (and if) necessary.

A Conversation with the Cook... "So often we think of liver fried up in a pan with onions and bacon, but I have found this to be a tasty variation for preparing liver and get compliments whenever I serve it. Have your butcher help you select a good carton of fresh, tender liver."

Oven Stew
Makes 6 Servings

2 pounds chuck beef, sliced
1 medium onion, sliced
4 potatoes
1 stalk celery
6 carrots
1 teaspoon salt
2 tablespoon tapioca
1 tablespoon sugar
1 cup tomato juice
2 bay leaves

Quarter potatoes; cut celery and carrots into chunks. Place in a buttered baking dish with the chuck beef and onion. Sprinkle with the salt, tapioca, and sugar. Pour tomato juice over stew and add bay leaves. Bake, covered, in slow oven at 300° for 4 hours. Remove bay leaves and serve.

A Conversation with the Cook... "Nothing tastes of comfort food more than a good beef stew on a cold winter's night. Serve leftovers the next night with a batch of freshly made buttered noodles."

"Dinner is not what you do
in the evening before something else.
Dinner is the evening."
Art Buchwald

Angie's Super Supper Roast
Makes 4 servings

1 (4 pound) chuck roast
2 large onions, coarsely cut
1 tablespoon brown sugar
1 teaspoon salt
1 teaspoon pepper
3 teaspoons catsup
2 tablespoons cider vinegar
2 bay leaves
16 ounces 7-Up®
1/2 cup raisins

Put meat in roasting pan. Add remaining ingredients. Bake in 350° oven. Turn from time to time. Bake until tender, about 2 hours. Remove bay leaves before serving. Add a big bowl of mashed potatoes to complete the meal.

A Conversation with the Cook... "Pungent, spicy, and slightly sweet this makes a great recipe for adults and kids alike."

Alicia's Baked Chop Suey

Makes 6 servings

1 pound ground beef
1 1/2 cups celery, chopped
1 cup chopped onion
3/4 cup water
1/2 cup Uncle Ben's® raw rice
1 (10.75 ounce) can cream of mushroom soup
1 (10.75ounce) can of cream of chicken soup
3 tablespoons soy sauce
Water as (and if) necessary
Cooked rice, at serving time
Crispy chow mein noodles for garnish, at serving time

Brown meat. While meat is browning, mix other ingredients in a bowl. Then add to the meat, mixing well. Transfer to a greased casserole dish and bake at 350° for 1 hour. After 30 minutes add a little water if it is necessary. Serve with rice and pass soy sauce and crispy chow mein noodles for garnish.

A Conversation with the Cook... "For fun try using chop sticks and don't forget fortune cookies at the end of the meal!"

MaryAnn's Magic Turkey Loaf
Makes 6 servings

3/4 cup coarsely-crushed corn flakes
1/4 cup Italian bread crumbs
3/4 cup milk
1/2 cup onion, chopped
1/2 cup green pepper, chopped
1/2 teaspoon ground sage
1/2 teaspoon salt
1/2 teaspoon pepper
1 teaspoon parsley flakes
1 pound of raw ground turkey
2 tablespoons brown sugar
1/4 cup catsup
1 teaspoon dry mustard
1/4 teaspoon dry nutmeg
1/8 teaspoon ground ginger

In a large bowl, combine the first 9 ingredients; mix well. Add ground turkey and blend thoroughly. Turkey mixture should be firm enough to shape, if not, add more bread crumbs. Shape into a loaf and put in a sprayed loaf-baking pan. Combine brown sugar, catsup, mustard, nutmeg, and ginger; pour over meat. Bake at 350°, uncovered, for 1 hour. Let set 5 minutes before slicing.

A Conversation with the Cook... "Don't let the long list of ingredients in this recipe scare you—it's really easier to make than it looks. Turkey makes a healthy option to the traditional ground-beef meat loaf and the touch of ginger and other spices gives this recipe its special flavor."

✧

Chicken Enchiladas
Makes 6 servings

2 (3 ounce) packages cream cheese
3 whole chicken breasts, cooked and shredded
1 tablespoon vinegar
1/2 cup sour cream
1 1/2 teaspoons prepared mustard
1/8 teaspoon salt
1/8 teaspoon garlic powder
1/4 cup pitted ripe olives, chopped
1 green pepper, ribbed, seeded, and chopped
Tabasco® sauce, to taste
8 corn tortillas, sautéed in a little cooking oil, and drained on paper towels
1 tablespoon olive or vegetable oil
1 (16 ounce) can stewed tomatoes
1 (8 ounce) can tomato sauce
2 tablespoons vegetable oil
2 avocados
1 cup Cheddar cheese, shredded

Soften cream cheese with vinegar; mix in sour cream, shredded chicken, mustard, salt, garlic powder, olives, green pepper, and a few drops Tabasco-style hot sauce. Set filling aside. Heat about 1 tablespoon oil in skillet; sauté tortillas, one at a time, lightly on each side; add more oil as necessary, until all tortillas have been cooked. Tortillas should not be crisp. Drain on paper towels.

In same skillet, heat tomatoes and tomato sauce with 2 additional tablespoons oil and a few drops of Tabasco® sauce. Meanwhile, spoon chicken mixture onto centers of tortillas. Spoon about 1 tablespoon tomato mixture over each; roll-up tortillas around filling. Place side by side and seam side down, in greased shallow 2-quart baking dish. Pour remaining hot tomato mixture over top. Cover lightly with foil. Bake in 400° oven 15 minutes, or until warmed through and bubbly. Cut avocados lengthwise into halves; remove pits and skin. Cut into slices; arrange on top of enchiladas. Sprinkle with Cheddar cheese and bake 3 minutes more, just to melt cheese but to not cook the avocados.

A Conversation with the Cook... "These Chicken Enchilladas are pretty labor intensive, but well worth the effort. They can be assembled ahead of time and stored in the fridge—just compensate with extra baking time. For an added treat serve with a garnish of sour cream and a salsa featured in Chapter Seven (see pages 220-222).

"The only really good
vegetable is Tabasco sauce."
P.J. O'Rourke

Impossible Taco Pie

Makes 6 servings

1 pound ground beef
1/2 cup chopped onion
1 (1.25 ounce) packet taco seasoning mix
1 (4 ounce) can chopped green chilies, drained
1 1/4 cups milk
3/4 cup Bisquick® baking mix
3 eggs
2 tomatoes, sliced
1 1/2 cups shredded Monterey Jack cheese
Sour cream, at serving time
Chopped tomatoes, at serving time
Shredded lettuce, at serving time
Chopped green onion, at serving time

Grease a 10-inch quiche dish or pie plate; set aside. Cook and stir beef and onion over medium heat until beef is brown; drain. Stir in seasoning mix. Spread in pie plate; sprinkle with chilies. With an electric mixer, beat milk, baking mix, and eggs until smooth. Pour over all in pie plate. Start baking in 350° oven for 25 minutes. Top with sliced tomatoes; sprinkle with cheese. Return to oven and bake 8 to 10 minutes longer. Cool 5 minutes before serving. Serve with sour cream and your favorite garnishes.

A Conversation with the Cook... "Make it hot and spicy; make it subtle and cheesy—this is a fun recipe to serve the whole family."

Poppy Seed Chicken
Makes 6 servings

6 cooked chicken breast halves, cubed
2 (10.75 ounce) cans cream of chicken soup
1 cup sour cream
3 "sleeves" Ritz® crackers, crushed into crumbs
3/4 cup butter, melted
2 1/2 tablespoons poppy seeds

Combine crumbs, butter, and poppy seeds. Put 1/2 of this cracker mixture into a greased 13 x 9-inch pan. Mix soup and sour cream with chicken and pour over crumbs. Add rest of crumbs on top of chicken mixture. Bake at 350° for 30 to 35 minutes. Serve with a nice salad and muffins to complete the meal.

A Conversation with the Cook... "Poppy seeds add a special touch to this dish; you can choose to add a little more or a little less to find your specific taste, but do add some."

Glenn's Salmon Casserole

Makes 6 servings

1 (8 ounce) package egg noodles
1 (16 ounce) can red salmon
1 small onion, diced
1 (10.75 ounce) can cream of celery soup
1 (8 ounce) can green peas
1/2 cup milk
1/4 teaspoon marjoram
Salt and pepper, on the dinner table

Cook noodles; drain. Gently fold in salmon, onion, soup, milk, and peas. Season mixture with marjoram and bake at 375° for 45 minutes in an oven-proof casserole dish. Serve with muffins or a bread from Chapter Eight.

A Conversation with the Cook... "Marjoram—may be used both dried and green. Use to flavor fish, poultry, and stews. Marjoram and salmon are automatic go-togethers."

Chapter Three
"Kitchen Klassics"
... by Classic Cooks

✧

"Tomatoes and oregano make it Italian
Wine and tarragon make it French
Sour cream makes it Russian
Lemon and Cinnamon make it Greek
Soy sauce makes it Chinese
Garlic makes it good."
~Alice May Brock

RECIPE INDEX

Sunday Roast Leg of Lamb, with Oven Roasted Potatoes and Gravy ... 71
Classic French Farmhouse Veal Roast ... 73
Dorothea's Clay Pot Meat Loaf ... 76
My Garden Stuffed Zucchini Boats ... 76
Mushroom Pie ... 78
Karls "Kuiche" ... 79
MAK and LOUISE (Scalloped Apple Noodle Bake) ... 80
Mrs. Dalle Ave's Beef Pastie Pie ... 81
Mom's Baked Glazed Ham ... 84
Donald's "Dogs" ... 85
Helga's Homemade Beef "Summer Sausage" ... 86

Grandma's Sicilian Meat Loaf ... 87
Stuffed Tomatoes ... 89
Stuffed Green Peppers ... 89
Old Fashioned Sausages and Sauerkraut ... 91
Glenn's Old Fashioned Taste Chicken Pot Pie ... 92
Countryside Chicken Bake ... 93
MaryAnn's Chicken Tetrazzini ... 94
Vegetarian Lasagna ... 96
Asparagus Quiche Lorraine ... 98
Easy Everyday Lasagna ... 99
Grandma Scherer's Side-by-Side Manicotti ... 100
MaryAnn's Pepper Steak ... 102
Suzanne's Cashew Chicken ... 103
Breanne's Chicken Cacciatore ... 104
Italian Roast Dinner ... 105
Taco Casserole ... 106

Sunday Roast Leg of Lamb with Oven Roasted Potatoes and Gravy

Serves a family of 4, with leftovers (for more, roast the whole leg)

Either half from a whole leg of lamb (I like U.S. lamb as opposed to New Zealand lamb)
Fresh garlic cloves
Salt and pepper
Baking potatoes, washed, peeled, and cut horizontally into quartered-wedges

Pierce about 8 or 9 incisions into the leg of lamb. Insert a peeled clove of garlic into each incision. (This will "infuse" a wonderful flavor of garlic throughout the meat.) Place fat side up in roasting pan. Bracket the meat with the potato wedges. Season all with salt and pepper before putting in oven. Bake at 325° for 30 minutes per pound. Turn potatoes half-way through cooking to brown and glaze in pan juices.

When done remove lamb to a warm platter and surround with potatoes. "Tent" (cover loosely) with foil and let rest 10 minutes before carving. While meat "rests" make gravy from pan juices. Put roasting pan on top of stove over medium heat. Skim off any extra fat that might be in the drippings. In a small lidded jar, shake together 1 or 2 tablespoons of flour with a small amount of water to form a smooth mixture (this will keep your gravy from turning lumpy as you thicken it). In another container have water handy, if you need to adjust back to thinner consistency.

Start to make gravy by gradually adding some of the flour/water thickener to the pan juices, stirring all the while. Stir to get up all the brown bits from bottom of pan, while gravy thickens. If gravy gets too thick add water (by small amounts), stirring constantly to arrive at desired consistency. When gravy is done, season to taste with salt and pepper. You can also add 1 or 2 teaspoons of Kitchen Bouquet® to darken and further flavor the gravy. Serve on the side, in a warm "sauceboat" (small gravy-dish) to pass. Keep any extra gravy warm in the pan, over low heat on the stove top. (There is nothing worse than cold gravy! So serve it in small amounts, and refill the gravy-boat as needed.)

A Conversation with the Cook... "Roast Lamb 101: Cooking for 30 minutes per pound yields a roast that is still pink in the center. (I prefer this to over-cooked grey-center, which dries out the lamb and makes it tough.) The extensive use of garlic gives the lamb a full-bodied, well-rounded taste that 'mellows-out' the 'wild-taste' that so many people associate with lamb. Many people 'disguise' their lamb with a garnish of mint-jelly, but I prefer the roasted potatoes and gravy as an accompaniment. I also like to offer the accent of my homemade Rose Wine Jelly (see page 231 for recipe) which is much more delicate than the mint jellies offered in the store. Have your butcher help you select a beautiful leg of U.S. lamb. Try cooking it this way, and I guarantee you won't be disappointed with this classic approach."

Classic French Farmhouse Veal Roast

Makes 6 servings

Roast:
1 (3 pound) veal roast
2 tablespoons butter
2 tablespoons oil
2 carrots, scrubbed and diced to 1/8-inch thick
2 onions, peeled and diced into 1/8-inch pieces
1/2 teaspoon salt
1/4 teaspoon pepper
2 or 3 tablespoons fresh parsley, chopped
1 to 2 bay leaves
Pinch of thyme
1/3 cup Madeira wine

Sauce:
1 cup beef stock
1 tablespoon cornstarch
2 tablespoons Madeira wine
2 tablespoons butter

In a Dutch oven or heavy oven-proof pot, brown roast quickly on all sides in the oil and butter on top of stove. Remove roast and reserve. Add the carrot and onion dice to the pot and sauté 10 minutes. Move vegetables to side and return roast to pot. Season with salt and pepper, and scoop half the sautéed vegetables over roast. Add the parsley, bay leaves, thyme, and Madeira. Tent the roast loosely with a domed layer of foil. Then put the cover on the pot. Transfer to a 325°

oven and bake "double-covered," 30 to 40 minutes per pound. When done, remove roast to platter and keep warm. Meanwhile bring pot back up to stove top and make sauce: Add 1 cup beef stock to the pot and boil 5 minutes. Blend cornstarch and wine together and add to pot. Stir and cook until thickened. Lastly swirl in 2 tablespoons of butter to "finish" sauce. Slice roast and serve with sauce.

A Conversation with the Cook... "An awesome recipe, I first enjoyed this dish in a country inn in France. Since veal is so expensive, I rarely make this classic dish—reserving it for special occasions and appreciative palates. Every time it takes me back to that little inn in France."

> *"The discovery of a new dish*
> *does more for the happiness of mankind*
> *than the discovery of a new star."*
> *Anthelme Brillat-Savarin*

Dorothea's Clay Pot Meatloaf
Makes 6 servings

Note: To make this dish, you will need an unglazed, lidded, clay cooking pot (such as a Nordic Ware® Lidded Oven Brique® Pot). You can find clay cooking pots at any fine gourmet outfitter.

1 pound ground beef
1 pound ground pork
1 onion, chopped
1/2 cup raisins, plumped
1 cup dry bread crumbs
2 tablespoons cognac
2 egg yolks
1/2 teaspoon nutmeg
Salt and pepper, to taste
2 egg whites, beaten stiff
2 tablespoons butter

Presoak both lid and bottom of clay pot in cold water for 10 minutes. While pot is soaking assemble meatloaf. Mix together beef through cognac—don't over work mixture. Slightly beat egg yolks with nutmeg, salt, and pepper. Add to meat mixture and blend. Beat egg whites stiff and gently fold into loaf mixture. Pour mixture into, buttered, dampened clay pot. Dot loaf with remainder of the 2 tablespoons butter. Put on cover and place pot in COLD oven. Close the door and turn on heat to 425°; bake 50 to 60 minutes. Do NOT open oven door; do NOT peek in pot—your patience will reward you.

A Conversation with the Cook... "A dear friend introduced me to clay pot cooking ... and I love it. Very easy, very fool proof, and yields a very wonderful melding of flavors! Based on an ancient style of cooking, our predecessors knew what they were doing!"

✧

My Garden Stuffed Zucchini Boats

Makes 4 to 6 servings, depending on the size of the zucchini

1 very, very large zucchini, that has escaped your attention in the garden and grown way, way too big
Butter

Filling:
2 cups diced, cooked lamb, cooked beef, or sautéed ground lamb, or sautéed lean ground beef
1 cup cooked rice of your choice (white, brown, or I like wild rice)
1 onion, diced
Salt and pepper to taste
2 to 3 cloves garlic, mashed and minced
Fresh parsley, chopped
Dash of cinnamon
Stewed tomatoes or tomato sauce, just to moisten and bind stuffing
Parmesan cheese

Halve lengthwise and hollow out center of a large zucchini, to make 2 long "boats." Discard hollowed-out pulp (it's mostly seeds). Sprinkle with salt and set to drain on paper toweling, just to de-hydrate a little (for about 10 minutes). Pat boats dry and spread with butter; brown under broiler for just a few minutes; set aside. Make a stuffing by sautéing meat through tomatoes in a little butter, to make a moist but packable filling. Mound warm filling directly into the broiled zucchini. Sprinkle with last ingredient, the Parmesan cheese. Bake at 375° for 45 minutes, or until filling is warmed through, and zucchini is fork tender but firm, and still holds its shape. (Baking time will vary with size of zucchini.) Cut into serving-size pieces and plate with fresh fruit on the side.

A Conversation with the Cook... "As a gardener, I have always been interested in ways to use up my zucchini—especially the ones that have been turning into giants, while hidden from my view! (You'd think I lived in Alaska, land of the giant vegetables!) I have made this versatile recipe with zucchini over 2 feet long, yet have used smaller store-bought ones also. The versatility of meat and rice choices for the stuffing also enhance this utilitarian dish. So the next time your neighbor offers you a zucchini the size of a baseball bat, take it, stuff it, bake it, and enjoy it!"

"He who plants a garden plants happiness."
Chinese Proverb

Mushroom Pie

Makes 8 serving-size wedges (or approximately 16 appetizer wedges)

1 (9-inch) pie shell, ready for baking
3 tablespoons butter
1 cup sliced onion
1 1/2 pounds fresh mushrooms, sliced
1 teaspoon salt
A few grinds of black pepper, from your pepper mill
1/2 teaspoon Worcestershire
1 tablespoon lemon juice
1/2 pound Swiss cheese, shredded
Butter
Parmesan cheese

To make filling, sauté butter and onion for 2 minutes. Add next 5 ingredients and sauté 5 minutes more. Drain off any excess liquid (as mushrooms are mainly made up of water) and toss with the shredded cheese. Fill a 9-inch pie shell. Dot with butter and sprinkle with Parmesan cheese. Bake at 375° for 35 to 40 minutes. Serve warm.

A Conversation with the Cook... "Serve hot or at room temperature for a luncheon or light alfresco dinner. Add a salad and good French bread or muffins to complete the meal. Or cut into thinner wedges and serve as fancy-finger-food hors d'eouvres (again warm or cold) with a glass of wine or an aperitif."

Karl's "Kuiche"

Makes 1 single-crust pie

1 ready-made pie crust, thawed
1/2 sweet onion, diced
4 ounces slab bacon, rind removed and chopped
2/3 cup whipping cream, chilled
2 tablespoons sour cream
1/3 cup sharp Cheddar cheese
Pepper to taste

In skillet brown bacon lightly; remove excess fat. Add onion; sauté till translucent. Set aside to cool. In food processor or with whisk, beat whipping cream with sour cream until soft peaks form. Fold in Cheddar cheese and add pepper; set aside. On flat cookie sheet, place crust and crimp edges up about 1/2-inch all around. Spread cream mixture level with edges. Sprinkle bacon mixture evenly on top of pie. Bake at 425° for 10 to 15 minutes, or until filling has set and both filling and topping are just beginning to brown. Serve warm.

A Conversation with the Cook... "This can be served as an entrée, or cut into finger-food size wedges to serve room-temperature as an appetizer."

MAK and LOUISE
(Scalloped Apple Noodle Bake)
Makes 6 to 8 servings

2 cups broad noodles
4 apples, peeled, cored, and sliced as if for pie
1/4 stick butter or margarine, melted
2 tablespoons sugar
Dash salt
Slight dash white pepper
Slight dash cinnamon
Sour cream, at serving time for garnish
Shredded Cheddar cheese

Boil noodles to al dente; rinse and drain well in colander. Meanwhile peel, pare, and cut apples into slices. Melt 1/4 stick butter and pour two thirds into bottom of Pyrex® style baking dish. Spread half the noodles in buttered dish. Then layer on the apples. Sprinkle apple layer with the sugar and a dash each: salt, white pepper, and cinnamon. Layer on remaining noodles. Drizzle top with last third butter. Cover with foil and begin baking at 350° for 10 minutes. Remove covering and continue baking 30 minutes more, or until apples are fork tender and top of casserole is golden brown. Let set 5 minutes before serving. Top each serving with a dollop of sour cream (or crème fraiche, see page 217) and a sprinkling of sharp Cheddar cheese.

A Conversation with the Cooks... "Made with ingredients we have on hand, this dish can be served at any meal of the day—a true comfort food for Sunday breakfast, brunch, lunch, a dinner side-dish, or even dessert. The next time you need to add an extra dish to your meal, try this old-fashioned one—you'll be asked for the recipe every time."

✧

Mrs. Dalle Ave's Beef Pastie Pie (pasties in single pie form)
Makes 4 to 6 hearty servings

Short Crust:
1 to 1 1/2 cups flour
1 teaspoon **each:** garlic salt and crushed oregano
1/4 cup Parmesan cheese
1/2 cup Crisco® shortening (or lard)
4 to 5 tablespoons ice water

Sift together flour, seasonings, and Parmesan cheese. Cut in shortening with a "pastry cutter" until blended to the size of small crumbles. With a fork, blend in 4 to 5 tablespoons of icy cold water to make a tender dough. Do NOT overwork the dough. Roll out half of the dough for bottom crust and half for the top crust.

A Conversation with the Cook... "If you don't feel like tackling homemade pie crust opt for a package of frozen pie shells—you will need two shells thawed, to fashion into a double-crust pie.(No one, but a pastie-gourmand will guess the difference between 'theirs' and 'yours.')"

Filling:
A nice slice of round steak, diced into cubes (trim out any sinew and fat)
Carrot, diced
Onion, diced
Potato, diced
Seasonings to taste of: salt, pepper, garlic powder, oregano, and parsley
1 to 2 tablespoons water, to moisten filling
Dots of butter, to top filling

Mix all but last 2 ingredients and generously season to taste. Mound onto bottom crust. Sprinkle filling with a little water. Dot with butter. Put on top crust and "crimp" around the edges to seal in filling. Pierce top crust a couple times to vent. Bake at 350° for 1 hour and 15 to 30 minutes—until crust is browned and filling is tender and steamy when pierced with fork. You will know when it's done, because it will smell wonderful.

A Conversation with the Cook... "These were originally made as individual, pudgy pies, hand-formed and crimped to hold their nutritious filling, to provide iron-miner husbands with a hot lunch to carry down into the dank, dark mines. Each pastie was lovingly wrapped in paper and packed in a special tin lunch bucket that had a tin-cup-compartment on the top to hold hot coffee or soup. The pastie would keep the coffee warm, and the coffee (or soup) would keep the pastie warm until lunch time.

Not feeling the need for quite so much crust, I like to make my pasties in a single-pie form, cutting it into serving-size wedges for all to enjoy. Originally made in Europe and brought over with the immigrants, this recipe is continued today all along the Iron Range of Michigan and Wisconsin. And the old-fashioned tin pastie-pails are prized as antique collectibles.

There are numerous variations to the recipe—but Mrs. Dalle Ave's is my favorite and I hope you will try it. She taught me to use lean round steak and cut all the filling-ingredients into uniformly small 1/4 -inch to 1/3 -inch dice. Other variations use ground meat, and some Cornish pies include turnips or cabbage, which I'm not fond of. The secret of incorporating oregano and Parmesan into my homemade short crust, gives the pie so much extra flavor."

"Our foods are a reflection of who we are,
where we've been, and what we do."
~Wendy Louise

Mom's Baked Glazed Ham
Flexible recipe; estimate 1/4 pound meat per person

1 fully cooked ham, from butcher counter
Whole cloves
1 cup brown sugar
3 tablespoons pan drippings, from the roasting ham
Set oven at 325° and bake ham according to following chart:
   Fully cooked half ham 15 to 17 minutes per pound
   Fully cooked whole ham 12 to 15 minutes per pound
   Canned ham, about 6 pounds, 20 minutes per pound
   Canned ham, about 8 to 13 pounds, 15 minutes per pound

Place ham fatty side up in heavy foil roasting pan. **(I like to use a disposable pan.)** With a knife, score fat in a diagonal criss-cross pattern. Stud with cloves. Calculate baking time according to above directions, or consult directions on the ham's packaging. During last 45 minutes of baking, frequently baste ham with a mixture of 1 cup brown sugar softened in 3 tablespoons of pan drippings. When ham is done, remove to platter for carving. Serve with Hot Fruit Compote (see page 207) on the side.

A Conversation with the Cook... "I like to make a ham for just about any occasion. It's easy and everybody likes a good ham. Select a little larger ham than you need, so you have plenty for leftovers. Serve initial ham roast with your favorite side dishes. Save leftover meat for sandwiches, or to be diced up in salads, omelets, or future casseroles. Utilize the bone for soup."

Donald's "Dogs"
Makes 10

1 package of 10 flour tortillas
1 package all beef bun-length hot dogs
A 2 to 4-ounce can diced green chilies
2 cups shredded Cheddar cheese
Taco sauce or salsa, at serving time

Lightly grease 9 x 13-inch glass baking dish. Wrap each hot dog in tortilla with approximately 1/4 cup cheese and generous amount of diced green chilies. Roll tightly until closed and place in baking dish side-by-side so you can line the rest up until the pan is full. They can be placed tightly together so they do not come open. When all dogs are wrapped, place in oven and bake at 350° until all of the cheese melts and the tortillas are golden brown (approximately 25 minutes). Serve with salsa or taco sauce.

A Conversation with the Cook... "You may also use turkey hot dogs. The full-length wraps may also be sliced into bite-size pieces, skewered with toothpicks, and served as an appetizer with salsa for dipping. Make some without the hot chilies for the kids."

Helga's Homemade Beef "Summer Sausage"

Makes 2 sausages

2 pounds ground hamburger meat
1 cup water
1 1/2 teaspoons Liquid Smoke®
1 1/2 teaspoons garlic powder
1 tablespoon mustard seed
1/2 teaspoon onion powder
A few whole pepper corns
2 tablespoons Morton Tender Quick Salt®
1 teaspoon table salt

Mix all ingredients and divide into 2 sausage-shaped logs. Wrap each in foil, shiny side next to meat. Refrigerate for 24 hours to set. Punch holes in the bottom of the foil (this will release drippings) and place on rack in a foil-lined pan (to catch the drippings). Bake at 350° for 1 1/2 hours. Cool; store cooked sausage in refrigerator. Slice and serve like summer sausage. Sausages can be frozen.

A Conversation with the Cook... "Okay, guys—this one's for you. Can't you just imagine serving your own homemade sausage at a tail-gating party or in hunting camp? I think this recipe would be great using ground venison! A true North-woods recipe, this was given to me by the wife of a lumberjack over 30 years ago. Her husband had cleared some land for me; I invited them for dinner and she brought this sausage as a 'hostess gift.'"

Grandma's Sicilian Meat Loaf

Makes 6 servings

2 pounds ground beef
8 thin slices ham
8 slices hard salami
2 eggs
3/4 cup soft bread crumbs
1/2 cup spaghetti sauce
1 1/2 teaspoons oregano
1 teaspoon garlic powder
1/2 teaspoon salt
1 teaspoon pepper
6 ounces shredded mozzarella cheese
3 slices mozzarella cheese

Mix ground beef, eggs, oregano, garlic powder, salt, pepper, and bread crumbs together. On aluminum foil, gently pat mixture into a 10 x 12-inch rectangle 1/2 -inch thick. Cover rectangle with ham slices, shredded mozzarella, and salami. Roll up; lift foil to roll. Seal ends tightly. Put in cake pan and bake, covered, at 350° for 1 hour. Uncover and top with 3 slices mozzarella and spaghetti sauce. Bake 30 minutes more.

A Conversation with the Cook... "Meat loaf just does not have to be an ordinary dish. Try this Sicilian Version or the Dorthea's Clay Pot recipe on page 76 and you will definitely take meat loaf from 'truck stop' to 'culinary.'"

Stuffed Tomatoes
Makes 6 servings

8 medium-size tomatoes, cored and trimmed
1 1/2 teaspoons olive oil, plus 1 tablespoon vegetable oil
1 onion, peeled and finely chopped
1/2 celery stalk, finely chopped
2 garlic cloves, smashed and chopped
1/2 pound lean ground beef
1 cup chopped tomatoes (reserved from trimming tomatoes)
3/4 cup cooked rice
1/2 teaspoon crushed oregano
1/2 cup grated Swiss cheese
Salt and Pepper, to taste

Preheat oven to 350°. Core tomatoes and place upside down on cutting board. Use sharp knife and slice off tops, either decoratively or plain. Scoop out most of the flesh (and reserve for later) but leave a solid shell; sprinkle insides with olive oil. Heat vegetable oil in sauce pan. When hot, add onion, celery, and garlic; cook 3 to 4 minutes over medium heat. Add in meat and season well; continue cooking 3 to 4 minutes. Add chopped tomatoes, rice, herbs, and spices to saucepan. Mix very well and cook 6 to 7 minutes over medium heat. Place tomato shells in greased baking dish and fill with meat mixture. Sprinkle with cheese and cook 25 minutes in 350° oven.

A Conversation with the Cook... "Add French bread and a nice salad, or serve alongside Corn Pudding (see page 196 to complete the meal."

Stuffed Green Peppers
Makes 4 servings

4 large green peppers or yellow peppers
1 1/2 tablespoons vegetable oil
1 small red onion, peeled and finely chopped
1 celery stalk, finely chopped
10 mushrooms, cleaned and finely chopped
1 garlic clove, smashed and chopped
A pinch **each:** salt and pepper
1 pound lean ground beef
1/2 teaspoon basil
1 1/2 cups chopped tomato
2 tablespoons tomato paste
1/2 cup grated Parmesan cheese
1 cup tomato juice
Additional salt and pepper, to season inside of peppers
1/2 cup brown sauce (your favorite brand)
Pinch of thyme

Place peppers standing-up on cutting board. Slice off tops and remove all seeds and fibers. Blanch (par-boil) peppers in salted boiling water 5 to 6 minutes. Cool under cold running water to stop cooking and hold color; set aside. Heat oil in large frying pan. When hot, add onion and celery; cover and cook 2 to 3 minutes over medium heat. Add mushrooms, garlic, salt, and pepper; mix well. Continue cooking 2 to 3 minutes, covered. Mix meat and basil and add to pan; cook 3 to 4 minutes, uncovered, over medium heat. Stir in chopped tomato and continue cooking 3 to 4 minutes uncovered, over medium heat. Add tomato paste and mix; cook filling 2 to 3 minutes more. Add cheese and mix well. Season inside of peppers with salt and pepper. Fill with meat mixture. Gently place filled peppers in baking dish, side by side and pour in tomato juice and brown sauce. Bake 30 to 35 minutes in 350° oven, until all is cooked, but peppers don't lose their shape.

A Conversation with the Cook... "Old fashioned, but never out of style, stuffed peppers make a wonderful entrée. Served with mashed potatoes or rice on the side, you have a very satisfying dinner for family or company."

Old Fashioned Sausages and Sauerkraut

Makes 8 servings

1 pound bacon, diced
1 small onion, peeled and diced
2 (19 ounce) cans sauerkraut, well drained
Pepper
1 or 2 whole cloves
1/4 cup dry white wine
1 cup cold water
1 1/2 bay leaves
8 **pre-cooked** sausages, preferably in natural casings
Pepper

Place diced bacon in ovenproof casserole that can also go on stove top; cook 2 to 3 minutes over low heat. Stir in onion and continue cooking, covered, 6 minutes over low heat. Add sauerkraut and mix well. Season well with pepper and add the cloves. Add wine, water, and bay leaves. Bring to boil. Put on cover and transfer to oven. Bake 2 hours at 350°. Slash fully cooked sausage's skins on the bias using sharp knife. This technique will prevent sausages from splitting and curling during heating in the casserole. Eight or 10 minutes before end of cooking, add sausages to the casserole, cover, and continue cooking.

A Conversation with the Cook... "A heavy Dutch oven is perfect to use for this dish. I like to use fully-cooked sausages for convenience."

Glenn's Old Fashioned-Taste Chicken Pot Pie

Makes 6+ servings

2 cups chicken, cooked and cubed
2 cups potatoes, cooked and cubed
2 cups frozen mixed vegetables, (cauliflower, broccoli, carrots), thawed
1 (10.75 ounce) can cream of chicken soup
1 (10.75 ounce) can cream of potato soup
1 cup milk
1/2 cup chopped onion
1/4 teaspoon dried thyme
1/4 teaspoon black pepper
1 (10 ounce) tube Hungry Jack® biscuits

In 3-quart oblong baking dish, combine soups, milk, thyme, and black pepper. Stir in vegetables, onions, and chicken. Bake mixture at 400° for 15 minutes. Meanwhile, cut each biscuit into quarters. Remove casserole from oven and stir. Arrange biscuit pieces over hot chicken mixture. Return casserole to oven and bake 15 minutes more, or until biscuits are golden brown and all is bubbly. Serve "family style" straight from the casserole.

A Conversation with the Cook... "Everything you need in one hearty dish and a way to use up left over chicken ... turkey would be good too."

Countryside Chicken Bake

Makes 4 servings

1 cup uncooked rice
1 cup celery slices
3/4 cup onion, chopped
1/2 teaspoon each: salt and pepper
1/4 cup fresh parsley, chopped
1 (10.75 ounce) can cream of mushroom soup
1/2 cup Miracle Whip® salad dressing
3/4 cup plus 1 tablespoon water
4 skinned chicken breast halves
A dusting of Hungarian paprika

Place rice in greased 13 x 9-inch baking dish. Cover with combined vegetables and seasonings. Combine soup and salad dressing, mixing well. Gradually mix water into soup mixture and pour 1/2 of the mixture over vegetables. Lay chicken breast halves on rice mixture and top with remaining soup mixture. Sprinkle with a dusting of paprika for color. Bake at 350° for 1 hour or until chicken is tender (and juices run clear) and rice is fully cooked.

A Conversation with the Cook... "Use sweet, smoky Hungarian paprika and you will never go back to any other kind! If you have one in your area—visit your specialty spice store to get the 'real stuff'—its taste is incomparable. If you don't have a specialty spice store available, check your market for the best sweet Hungarian paprika on the shelf. You won't be sorry you made the extra effort."

MaryAnn's Chicken Tetrazzini
Makes 6 servings

1/2 cup butter
2 cups cubed cooked chicken, or turkey
6 ounces spaghetti, cooked
1 (10.75 ounce) can cream of chicken soup
1 (10.75ounce) can cream of mushroom soup
2 (4 ounce) cans sliced mushrooms, drained
1 cup shredded Cheddar cheese, divided
1 cup sour cream
3/4 cup sliced almonds
1/2 cup Parmesan cheese
1 teaspoon minced onion

Melt butter; combine with soups and mix well; add mushrooms, cooked-cubed chicken (or turkey), 1/2 cup Cheddar cheese, spaghetti, onion, and sour cream. Pour into 13 x 9-inch pan; sprinkle with Parmesan cheese, remaining 1/2 cup Cheddar cheese, and almonds. Bake at 350° uncovered for 30 to 40 minutes, till heated through, bubbly, and top is golden.

A Conversation with the Cook... "This is a fabulous way to use up leftover chicken, or during the holidays, leftover turkey. Kind on the taste buds and kind on the pocketbook, it's almost like getting a bonus meal from leftovers and items pulled from your pantry."

"The most remarkable thing about my mother is that for 30 years she served the family nothing but leftovers. The original meal has never been found."
~Calvin Trillin

Vegetarian Lasagna
Makes 6+ servings

1 (1 pound) package lasagna noodles
3 tablespoons butter
1 onion, peeled and diced small
3 carrots, pared and diced small
1/2 head of fresh cauliflower, chopped
1 green pepper, ribbed, seeded and diced fine
1/2 of a tender zucchini, diced fine
Salt and pepper, to taste
2 tomatoes, cored and diced fine
1 /2 pound mushrooms, cleaned and diced
1 tablespoon grated lemon rind
1/4 teaspoon nutmeg
1/2 teaspoon ground clove
1 teaspoon oregano
1/4 teaspoon thyme
1 cup grated Gruyere cheese
1 cup grated Mozzarella cheese
4 cups white sauce, heated (use basic recipe on page 198)
Salt and pepper to taste

Butter 13 x 9-inch lasagna dish; set aside. Cook pasta in plenty of boiling salted water with a bit of oil added. Be sure pot is wide enough to allow noodles to lie flat. Follow directions on package and remove pasta when done. Drain pasta and rinse in cold water to stop cooking. Carefully separate the noodles and lay out on paper towels. Cover with more paper towels, until ready to use. Heat butter in large saucepan. When hot, add onion; cover and cook 3 minutes over low heat.

Add carrots and mix; continue cooking covered for 3 to 4 minutes over low heat. Add cauliflower, green pepper, and zucchini; season generously with salt and pepper to taste. Cover and cook 4 to 5 minutes more over low heat. Stir in tomatoes, mushrooms, lemon rind, and spices; cover and continue cooking an additional 3 to 4 minutes. Remove saucepan and set aside. Meanwhile prepare white sauce according to instructions on page 198 and set aside. Arrange first layer of pasta in lasagna dish. Add layer of vegetables, layer of cheese, and layer of warmed white sauce. Repeat until most of ingredients are used. Finish with layer of pasta. Top with remaining sauce and cheese. Bake 45 minutes in 375° oven, or until all is hot and bubbly. Let set 5 minutes before slicing and serving.

A Conversation with the Cook... "Reserve any leftovers, which reheat easily in oven, for a next-day-snack. Lasagna is a great 'next day' food as its flavor seems to get even better."

A Special Conversation about Pasta... "Pasta can be tricky, and sticky, and over-cooked. When using in a casserole cook your pasta just until 'al dente' (which means 'still has a tooth') or just until about done, but still a little chewy. Pasta will continue to cook in your casserole and you don't want it to become too soft—so the order of the day is to under-cook it just a little when prepping—allowing for additional cooking in the casserole."

Asparagus Quiche Lorraine
Makes 6 servings

1 unbaked pie shell
3/4 cup diced cooked chicken
1/4 cup finely diced ham
1 1/4 cups shredded Swiss cheese
2 cups cooked asparagus, cut 1/2-inch size
3 eggs
Milk
Nutmeg
Pepper

Place cooked chicken and ham in pie shell. Arrange shredded cheese evenly over all. Break eggs into a large measuring cup; add milk to level of 1 1/4 cup marker. Add a pinch of nutmeg and a dash of pepper. Beat well with fork. Pour mixture into pie shell. Top with cooked asparagus. Bake at 425° for 15 minutes. Reduce heat to 300° and continue baking 30 to 40 minutes more, or until knife inserted in center comes out clean. Let set 5 minutes before slicing into wedges to serve.

A Conversation with the Cook... "Classically French, classically delicious with its mélange of flavors, this special recipe is a favorite at our house. The hint of nutmeg is a must."

Easy Everyday Lasagna
Makes 6 servings

1 pound ground beef
2 tablespoons olive oil
1 (8 ounce) can tomato sauce
1 (15 ounce) can whole tomatoes
1 1/2 teaspoon salt
1 pound cottage cheese
1/2 teaspoon garlic salt
1/2 teaspoon crushed oregano
1/2 teaspoon pepper
1/2 pound shredded mozzarella cheese
1/2 cup grated Parmesan cheese
9 lasagna noodles

Brown ground beef in oil; add tomatoes, salt, and spices; simmer 20 minutes, breaking up tomatoes with the back of a wooden spoon. Cook 9 lasagna noodles until tender; drain and rinse. Fill a non-stick sprayed 13 x 9-inch baking pan with alternate layers of noodles, shredded cheese, and meat sauce. Top with grated Parmesan. Bake at 375° for 20 minutes.

A Conversation with the Cook... "A quick and easy lasagna that is good for everyday meals and kid-friendly."

Grandma Scherer's Side-by-Side Manicotti

Makes 6 servings

1 (12 to 14 tubes) box manicotti
1 pound Italian sausage
1 (15 ounce) tub ricotta cheese
1 (8 ounce) package Mozzarella cheese, divided
1/2 cup Parmesan cheese, divided
1 cup mushrooms, chopped
4 green onions, chopped
1/2 cup green pepper, chopped
2 eggs, each beaten lightly individually
1 teaspoon dried oregano
2 teaspoons garlic powder, divided
1 teaspoon fennel seed
Salt and pepper to taste
1 (32 ounce) jar spaghetti sauce (your favorite brand)

Boil manicotti according to package directions; drain and set aside. In a medium bowl, mix ricotta cheese, green onions, green pepper, 1 egg, 1/4 cup Parmesan cheese, oregano, 1 teaspoon garlic powder, and mushrooms. Stuff 1/2 of the tubes with this mixture. In skillet, fry Italian sausage and crumble into small pieces. Remove and drain grease. Add 4 ounces mozzarella, the fennel seed, second teaspoon garlic powder, and second egg; mix and stuff remaining tubes. In a casserole dish, spread a thin layer of spaghetti sauce. Place filled manicotti tubes side by side, alternating cheese and meat tubes, into the casserole dish. Spread remaining sauce over tubes and sprinkle remaining cheeses. Cover with foil and bake for 30 minutes at 350°, until all is heated through and bubbly. Make sure each serving gets "one of each."

A Conversation with the Cook... "What can I say...this dish speaks for itself."

MaryAnn's Pepper Steak
Makes 6 servings

1 1/2 pounds top beef round or sirloin steak, 1-inch thick slice
1/4 cup olive oil
1 cup water
1 medium onion, cut into 1/4-inch slices
1/2 teaspoon garlic salt
1/8 teaspoon ginger
2 green peppers, ribbed, seeded, and cut into 3/4-inch strips
1 tablespoon cornstarch
2 teaspoons sugar
2 tablespoons soy sauce
2 medium tomatoes

Trim fat from meat; cut meat into strips, 2 x 1/4-inch. Heat oil in large skillet. Cook meat strips quickly in oil, turning frequently, until brown, about 5 minutes. Stir in water, onion, garlic, and ginger; heat to boiling. Place mixture in baking dish, cover, and bake at 350° for 15 minutes. Add green pepper strips during the last 5 minutes. Meanwhile over medium heat, blend cornstarch, sugar, and soy sauce. Cook, stirring constantly until mixture thickens and boils. Pour over baking meat mixture and stir all to blend. Cut tomatoes into eighths; place on meat mixture. Cover and continue baking just until tomatoes are heated through, about 5 minutes more. Serve over hot cooked rice.

A Conversation with the Cook... "Meat will be succulent and tender, sauce rich in flavor, green peppers tender-crisp, and tomatoes fresh and colorful."

Suzanne's Cashew Chicken
Makes 4 to 6 servings

1 (3 to 4 pound) broiler/fryer chicken, cut up and skin removed
1 medium onion, thinly sliced
1/2 cup orange juice concentrate
1 teaspoon dried rosemary, crushed
1/2 teaspoon salt
1/4 teaspoon cayenne pepper
2 tablespoon all-purpose flour
3 tablespoon water
1/2 cup chopped cashews
Hot cooked pasta or rice, at serving time

Place chicken pieces in a baking dish. Combine onion, orange juice concentrate, rosemary, salt, and cayenne pepper; pour over chicken. Cover and bake at 325° for 2 hours or until chicken juices run clear, and chicken is falling off the bone. Remove chicken to a serving platter and keep warm. (Reserve all cooking juices that remain in the baking pan.) In saucepan, combine flour and water until smooth. Stir in cooking juices from the baking dish. Bring to a boil; cook and stir for 2 minutes or until thickened. Stir in cashews. Pour sauce over chicken. Serve with hot cooked pasta or rice.

A Conversation with the Cook... "This elegant entrée with fresh herb flavor is mouth-watering. Cashews add richness and crunch."

Breanne's Chicken Cacciatore
Makes 6 servings

1 (2 1/2 to 3 pound) broiler/fryer chicken, cut up and skin removed
2 medium onions, thinly sliced
2 garlic cloves, minced
1/2 teaspoon salt
1 teaspoon pepper
2 teaspoons dried oregano
1/2 teaspoon dried basil
1 bay leaf
1 (14.5 ounce) can diced tomatoes
1 (8 ounce) can tomato sauce
1 cup fresh mushrooms, sliced
1/2 cup dry white wine, water, or chicken broth
Hot cooked pasta, at time of serving

Place sliced onions in bottom of baking dish. Top with chicken pieces, then seasonings, tomatoes, sauce, mushrooms, and wine (or water) in that order. Cover; bake at 325° for 3 hours. Discard bay leaf before serving. Serve chicken with pan sauces over hot cooked pasta.

A Conversation with the Cook... "Breanne's recipe is very easy to make, but is also special enough to serve to company. Start the dish on a lazy afternoon and let its wonderful aromas fill your house with home-cooked goodness. Meanwhile you have 3 hours to watch a good movie or whip up a fabulous dessert from Chapter Nine."

Italian Roast Dinner
Makes 8 to 10 servings

1 (3 to 4 pound) boneless rump roast
1/2 teaspoon salt
1/2 teaspoon garlic powder
1/2 teaspoon pepper
1 (4.5 ounce) can sliced mushrooms, drained
1 medium onion, diced
1 (15 ounce) can spaghetti sauce (your choice of brand)
1/4 cup beef broth
Hot cooked pasta of choice, at serving time

Cut the roast in half. Combine salt, garlic powder, and pepper; and evenly rub over roast. Place in a casserole dish. Top with mushrooms and onion. Combine the spaghetti sauce and broth; pour over meat and vegetables. Cover and bake at 325° for 3 1/2 hours, or until meat is fork tender. Slice roast; serve over pasta of choice with pan juices.

A Conversation with the Cook... "This is a deliciously different Italian-style main dish."

Taco Casserole

Makes 6 servings

1 pound ground beef
1 (8 ounce) can Bush's® chili beans, drained
1 (8 ounce) can tomato sauce
2 to 4 teaspoons chili powder, to taste
2 tablespoons taco sauce
1 teaspoon garlic salt
2 cups tortilla chips, broken into pieces
1 cup sour cream
1/2 cup sliced green onions
1 large tomato, chopped
1 cup shredded Cheddar cheese

At time of serving:
Additional tortilla chips
Shredded lettuce
Taco sauce
Black olives

Cook and stir ground beef in skillet until brown, drain. Stir in beans, tomato sauce, taco sauce, chili powder, garlic salt, and heat. Place chips in un-greased 2 quart casserole. Top with beef mixture. Spread with sour cream, sprinkle with onions, tomato, and cheese. Bake uncovered at 350° until hot and bubbly, 20 to 30 minutes. Arrange additional tortilla chips around edge of casserole. Serve with shredded lettuce, taco sauce, and black olives for garnish.

A Conversation with the Cook... "MaryAnn's recipe provides all the taste of a taco, with the ease of a casserole."

*"At a loss for words?
Consider good-cooking 'edible-conversation.'"
~Wendy Louise*

Chapter Four
"Company's coming for dinner ... Let's Get Fancy"

✧

"If more of us valued food and cheer and song above hoarded gold, it would be a merrier world."
~J.R.R. Tolkien, writer

Recipe Index

Yorkshire Chicken Bake ... 111
Wild Wild-Rice Chicken Bake ... 112
Chicken in a Clay Pot ... 114
Clay Pot Pork Roast ... 116
Budin Chicken Tortilla Bake ... 117
Divine Chicken Divan ... 119
    Bonus-Recipe Chicken Broccoli Crepes ... 121
Mom's Chicken Royale ... 122
Enchiladas Acapulco ... 124
Auntie Joan's Crab Carib ... 126
Barbara's Venetian Veal Pie ... 128
Oven Roasting Beef 101 ... 131
Madeira Sauce (for roasted meats) ... 132
Traditional Roast Turkey with Pan Gravy
  and Stuffing-on-the-Side ... 133
Mediterranean Pot Roast ... 141
Peach-Stuffed Chicken Breasts ... 142

Red Snapper with Garden Sauce ... 144
Roast Cornish Hens ... 145
Stuffed Crown Roast of Pork ... 147
My Pork Chops with Tomato-Olive Sauce ... 149
Grandma Scherer's Baked Tenderloin ... 150
Suzanne's Glazed Pork Tenderloin ... 151
Chicken Bake No Peek ... 152
New Orleans-Style Chicken ... 153
Glenn's Stuffed Pork Chops ... 155
Hawaiian Spareribs ... 156
Mary's Roast Rib-Eye ... 157
Braised Rib-Eye Steaks ... 158

Yorkshire Chicken Bake

Makes 6 servings

Casserole:
1 broiler-fryer chicken, cut up
1/4 cup oil
1/3 cup flour
2 teaspoons salt
1/4 teaspoon pepper
1 1/2 teaspoons crumbled leaf-sage

Yorkshire Pudding for Topping:
1 cup flour
1 teaspoon baking powder
1 teaspoon salt
1 1/2 cups milk
3 eggs
4 teaspoons crumbled parsley flakes

Pour oil into 9 x 13-inch baking dish. Combine flour, salt, pepper, and sage in a pie tin. Dredge chicken pieces in flour mixture to coat well. Rub each coated chicken piece, skin side down in the oil in the baking dish; turn over and arrange in single layer. Bake chicken at 400° for 40 minutes. While chicken bakes prepare Yorkshire pudding for topping: Sift together flour, baking powder, and salt into a medium-size bowl. Gradually beat in milk, eggs, and parsley, to form a smooth batter. Place the cooking-chicken-dish on a foil-lined cookie sheet to catch any overflow. Pour Yorkshire Pudding over chicken. Return dish (now on the cookie sheet) to oven to bake for 20 to 25 minutes more, or till puffed and brown. Do NOT open oven door while topping is baking, or topping will not puff. Remove from oven and serve immediately.

A Conversation with the Cook... "It is very important to not disturb the casserole once you've put the Yorkshire pudding on top."

✧

Wild Wild-Rice Chicken Bake
Makes 4 servings

4 boneless, skinless chicken breast halves
2/3 cup raw wild rice, rinsed and drained
1/4 cup minced onion
1/4 cup chopped green bell pepper
2 cups sliced celery
1 1/2 cups water
2 chicken bouillon cubes
1/2 teaspoon salt
Soy sauce or Teriyaki sauce

Mix ingredients 2 through 7 and place in greased 2-quart baking dish. Lay chicken breasts on top of rice mixture. Brush each chicken breast with soy sauce or teriyaki sauce. Cover tightly with lid or foil and bake for 1 1/2 hours at 350° or until chicken is cooked through and rice has absorbed liquid and is puffed and tender.

A Conversation with the Cook... "Coming from wild rice country, I had to include a recipe with this wonderfully-chewy nutty-flavored grain. The use of Soy or Teriyaki sauce on the chicken enriches its flavor to make a nice balance with the boldness of the wild rice.

Many years ago I was privileged to attend an Ojibwa Wild Rice Pow Wow—a festival of drums and dancing, foods and costumes to celebrate the Wild Rice Moon and the coming harvest of 'the good grain that grows on water.' Considering the grain a sacred gift, Native Americans still harvest the rice in their ancient manner of poling a flat bottom boat through the shallow reeds, while another person beats the grain off the stalks with two smooth sticks and lets it gather in the bottom of the boat.

The majority of the wild rice found in our markets today has been turned over to commercially grown grain from 'wild rice marshes (or farms)' and processed in bulk for grocery markets ... much like our cranberry harvests of today, that once grew wild in the great North Woods in smaller quantities for 'those in the know' to enjoy."

Chicken in a Clay Pot

Makes 4 to 6 servings

Note: To make this dish, you will need an **unglazed,** lidded, clay cooking pot (such as a Nordic Ware® Lidded Oven Brique® Pot). You can find clay cooking pots at any fine gourmet outfitter, or in specialty cooking catalogues.

1 (3 pound) chicken, left whole
1 tablespoon butter
1 onion, diced
1 clove garlic, minced
2 carrots, diced
2 stalks celery, de-veined and diced
1 fresh lemon, juice and grated peel
1/4 cup cooking Vermouth
1/4 cup chicken broth
1/2 teaspoon salt
1/4 teaspoon pepper
Paprika, optional

Soak both bottom and top of clay pot in water for 10 minutes. Place diced onion, garlic, carrots, and celery in bottom of pot. Place pat of butter in chicken's cavity and place chicken on the vegetables. Add to the pot, the lemon juice and peel, Vermouth, and chicken broth. Season with salt and pepper. You can sprinkle the chicken with a little paprika if you wish, for color. Cover with lid and place in a COLD oven. Close oven door; turn on heat setting to 450° and bake, undisturbed, for 1 1/2 hours. Carve and serve straight from the pot. Use cooking juices "as is" over the chicken and a side of mashed potatoes.

A Conversation with the Cook... "Do NOT peek; do NOT open oven door; do NOT remove lid—have faith in the process. At the end of the hour and a half, ceremoniously remove the lid to reveal the most succulent chicken you've ever tasted. It will be falling-from-the-bone tender and beautifully browned. I like to use the juices just as they are, although I suppose they could be thickened into gravy."

Clay Pot Pork Roast
Makes 6 servings

Note: To make this dish, you will need an **unglazed,** lidded, clay cooking pot (such as a Nordic Ware® Lidded Oven Brique® Pot). You can find clay cooking pots at any fine gourmet outfitter, or in specialty cooking catalogues.

1 (3+ pound) bone in, loin pork roast
Salt and freshly cracked black pepper
1 teaspoon dried sage
1 teaspoon dried crumbled parsley
2 bay leaves

Soak entire clay pot in water for 10 minutes. While pot is soaking, rub salt and freshly cracked pepper into the surface of the roast. Place pork roast in the pot, bone side down. Rub surface of roast with dried sage and parsley. Throw 2 bay leaves into the pot. Cover with lid and put in COLD oven. Close oven door and turn heat setting to 450°; bake UNDISTURBED for 1 1/2 hours. Serve with your favorite apple sauce on the side (I like to make homemade...see page 215).

A Conversation with the Cook... "Clay Pots require minimal maintenance and cleaning. Follow suggestions in the booklet that comes with your pot. The more you use your pot the darker and built-up with 'patina' it will get, but it should serve you well for a lifetime of specialty cooking."

Budin Chicken Tortilla Bake
Makes 6 to 8 servings

12 to 16 soft-flour (Americanized taste) or soft-corn (for authentic Mexican taste) tortillas
3 cups cooked chicken, shredded
1 1/2 cups sour cream
2 cups shredded Cheddar cheese
3 tablespoons Canola oil
2 cups tomato sauce
1 cup Mexican tomato sauce with chilies
2 cloves garlic, mashed and minced
1/4 teaspoon sugar
1/8 teaspoon cinnamon
1/2 teaspoon salt, dash of pepper
1/3 onion, chopped
1/2 cup water

On stove top, in 3 tablespoons of Canola oil, heat and blend the last 8 ingredients listed to make a sauce; set aside. Layer a greased 9 x 13–inch baking dish with 1/3 of the tortillas, then 1/2 of the chicken, followed by 1/3 sauce, 1/3 sour cream, 1/3 cheese. Repeat. Top with last 1/3's each: tortillas, sauce, sour cream, and finally cheese. Bake on center rack in 350° oven until "budin" is heated through, bubbly, and cheese has melted on top—about 30 to 35 minutes. Let stand 10 minutes to set before serving. Serve with optional Avocado Sauce, (see page 216 for recipe) and pass an extra garnish of sour cream.

A Conversation with the Cook... "This makes a great company-coming-to-dinner dish because it can be assembled 2 hours in advance and stored in fridge. If putting in oven directly from fridge add to your cooking time by 10 to 15 minutes to compensate for coldness."

Divine Chicken Divan
Makes 8 servings

Meat:
1 chicken
1 tablespoon salt
6 peppercorns
1 onion, quartered
Celery leaves (from one or two stalks)
2 or 3 sprigs parsley
Water

Sauce:
1/3 cup butter
6 tablespoons flour
2 cups reserved chicken broth
3/4 cup heavy cream
2 tablespoons Sherry
Salt and pepper to taste

Vegetable:
1 bunch fresh broccoli, trimmed, cut, and separated into stalks with flowerets
Water
Pinch of salt
1/4 cup Parmesan cheese, at assembly time

(1) Poach chicken with seasonings and water to cover for 45 minutes. Remove chicken from boiling water, cool, remove meat from bones, and set aside. Reserve 2 cups of the broth and set aside.

(2) In saucepan make a sauce by starting with a roux of flour and butter, stirred and cooked to make a "paste." Slowly add reserved 2 cups of broth and heavy cream. Simmer, stirring, for 2 minutes. Cool. Stir in Sherry and season to taste with salt and pepper. Set aside.

(3) Cut tough bottoms off broccoli and trim into 3 or 4 -inch individual stalks, with their flowerets on top. Poach in salted water for 10 minutes. Remove from boiling water and rinse with cold water to stop cooking. Drain well and set aside. (All 3 of these steps can be made in advance, and casserole assembled, wrapped and stored in fridge until cooking time. If doing so, remove casserole from fridge and let stand 15 minutes to bring to room temperature while oven is preheating Pop into oven and cook per instructions.)

(4) To assemble, arrange broccoli to cover bottom of 9 x 13-inch, buttered baking dish. Line up in two rows, placing floweret-ends toward the outside, stalk-ends toward the center. Pour on 1/2 of sauce. Arrange chicken down center of casserole, over broccoli, covering the stalks but letting flowerets peek out the sides. (This will make the casserole pretty.) Add 1/4 cup Parmesan cheese to remaining sauce and pour over chicken.

(5) Bake at 375° until hot and bubbly. Put under broiler for 2 minutes to brown sauce. Put casserole on hot pad on the table, and serve directly from the casserole. Add a side dish of rice pilaf and a favorite salad

from the "Outside the Oven" Chapter to complete the meal.

A Conversation with the Cook... "This was my very-first-ever special meal that I made for company and it remains one of my favorites to this day!"

Bonus-Recipe Chicken-Broccoli Crepes

A batch of crepes (French pancakes—I have not included pancake batter recipe—use your favorite)
Steps 1, 2, and 3 from previous recipe to fill the crepes

Alter Chicken Divan Recipe to Crepe Recipe by rolling crepes (jelly roll fashion) each around a filling of 1 broccoli stalk and a generous amount of chicken for each. Pour 1/3 of white sauce in bottom of 9 x 13-inch buttered casserole dish. Arrange filled crepes, side by side, on sauce in single layer. Mix the Parmesan with remaining sauce and pour over crepes. (Like previous recipe, this can be assembled ahead of time, stored in fridge, pulled-out and baked at dinnertime.) Bake at 375° until heated through and bubbly. Finish off under broiler for 2 minutes to brown sauce. Serve.

A Conversation with the Cook... "When you have gone to all the effort to make these incredible dishes, be sure to serve on warmed dinner plates. Place stack of plates in a just-turned-off oven, and let warm while you are bringing your foods (hot and piping) to the table."

Mom's Chicken Royale
Makes 4 large servings

4 chicken breasts, boned and butterflied (see page 143)
Flour
1/2 teaspoon salt
1/2 teaspoon paprika
1/4 teaspoon white pepper
2 cups prepared bread stuffing (I like Pepperidge Farms®)
Toothpicks
1 stick butter, melted
1 box mushrooms, sliced
1/4 cup diced onion
2 tablespoons butter
2 tablespoons flour
1/2 cup cream
1/2 cup sour cream
1/2 teaspoon salt
1/4 teaspoon white pepper

Have butcher butterfly chicken breasts for you. Put flour, salt, paprika, and white pepper in a paper bag and shake to mix. Add chicken breasts (one at a time) and shake in bag to coat evenly. Mound 1/2 cup stuffing on one side of breast, fold over other side to enclose filling and secure all around edge with toothpicks to hold in filling. Filled breasts will be very plump. Place chicken breasts in 9 x 13-inch Pyrex® baking dish. Pour on the melted butter. Bake for 1 1/2 hours at 325°, turning breasts over half way through. When chicken is almost done, in a separate saucepan make a "royale" sauce. Start by sautéing the mushrooms and onion in 2 tablespoons butter until golden. Whisk in the flour to thicken. Add cream, sour cream, salt, and white pepper, whisking all the while to make smooth rich sauce. Heat sauce thoroughly, but do not boil! Remove baking dish from oven and pour the sauce directly over the chicken. Bring the dish to the table and serve chicken directly from dish, spooning sauce and cooking juices over each serving.

A Conversation with the Cook... "Once cream and/or sour cream have been added to a sauce, never let it boil. If you do, the sauce might curdle—this is called 'breaking' and is not desirable."

> *"Cookery has become a noble art,*
> *a noble science..."*
> *~Robert Burton*

Enchiladas Acapulco

Makes 12 servings

12 large flour tortillas, slightly warmed

Filling:
2 tablespoons butter
2 cups cooked chicken
3/4 cup pitted black olives, chopped
3/4 cup slivered almonds
1 cup shredded Cheddar cheese

Sauce:
1 quart chicken broth
4 tablespoons chili powder
Garlic powder, salt, and pepper, to taste
Dashes cinnamon and cumin
2 tablespoons cornstarch
4 tablespoons water

Topping:
1+ cup shredded Cheddar cheese

Garnish:
Sour cream, at time of serving
Chopped green onion, including tops, at time of serving
Additional black olives, at time of serving

(1) Mix and heat filling-ingredients in butter, in skillet, to blend flavors and melt cheese; set aside.

(2) To make sauce bring chicken broth to a boil and add seasonings to taste. Shake cornstarch and water in a small lidded jar to dissolve, and add to saucepan. Boil sauce 1 or 2 minutes to thicken; set aside.

(3) To assemble casserole, spread each tortilla with a little warm sauce. Mound with 1/12th of the chicken mixture. Roll up. Place rolls side by side in a greased 9 x 13-inch baking dish. Spread with a little more sauce and top with 1+ cup Cheddar cheese (make it as cheesy as you like).

(4) Bake in 350° oven until all is heated through and cheese has melted.

(5) Keep remaining sauce warm and spoon onto each serving as meal is plated; garnish with sour cream, chopped green onion, and black olives.

A Conversation with the Cook... "Remember all your ingredients have been pre-cooked, so you're only baking your finished casserole to warm it through, blend flavors, and have it become melty-good. This 'double-cooking' of the ingredients is what makes the finished product doubly-tasty!"

"Make food; not war."
~Wendy Louise

Auntie Joan's Crab Carib

Makes 8 luncheon or light-dinner servings

4 avocados, ripe but firm, halved and pitted, left in shells, and sprinkled with a little lemon or lime juice to prevent discoloring; covered with plastic wrap until ready to use

Stuffing:
3 tablespoons butter
3 tablespoons flour
1 1/4 cups half-and-half cream
1 teaspoon salt
1/8 teaspoon white pepper
Dash of Tabasco
2 tablespoons capers
1 pound cooked crab meat

Topping:
1/2 cup Cheddar cheese, grated (and to be divided amongst the 8 servings)

To make stuffing, start in a saucepan, with a roux (a blended and smooth paste) of melted butter and flour. Stir in the cream and gently cook and stir to thicken. Add seasonings and stir. Fold in capers and crabmeat and stir again to mix all. Arrange prepared avocado halves in a greased 9 x 13-inch baking dish. Mound each avocado-half with 1/8 of stuffing and sprinkle with 1/8 of cheese, covering entire top of avocado. Bake at 375° for just 20 minutes, to warm the filling and melt the cheese. Be careful not to overcook! as you want to warm **just** the stuffing and not really the avocados. Carefully transfer to serving plates; serve immediately with the accompaniments of a nice salad and crusty French bread or muffins.

A Conversation with the Cook... "There's an old saying amongst tennis players—'When you play with a player better than you, you automatically raise your game.' You automatically play better. It's the same with cooking—some of your best recipes are 'tried and trues' you've gotten from your best friends, or a relative. You automatically cook better! This is one of those recipes."

Barbara's Venetian Veal Pie

Makes 6 servings

Short Crust:
1 1/2 cup flour
1 teaspoon garlic salt
1 teaspoon crushed oregano
1/4 cup Parmesan
1/2 cup butter, cut into pieces
4 to 5 tablespoons ice water

Filling:
1 pound veal, cut into bite-size pieces
1/2 cup flour
1/4 cup butter
2 cups chopped tomatoes
1 cup tomato sauce
1/4 cup chopped onion
1/2 teaspoon each: salt, minced garlic, crushed oregano
3 tablespoons Parmesan cheese
1 tablespoon sugar
1 teaspoon crushed basil

Topping for Filling:
1/4 pound Cheddar cheese, shredded

(1) To make crust, sift together flour and spices. With a pastry cutter, cut in butter till dough is crumbly. With tines of fork, work in 4 to 5 tablespoons of icy cold water, 1 tablespoon at a time. Work gently and do not overwork the dough. Roll out 1/2 dough on

floured surface to make bottom crust. Reserve remaining dough.

(2) Make filling by, dredging veal pieces in flour and sauté in the butter till browned on all sides. Add remaining ingredients (tomatoes through crushed basil) and simmer gently for 30 minutes to meld flavors.

(3) Place bottom crust in pie plate. Turn filling into pie shell. Sprinkle liberally with 1/4 pound shredded Cheddar cheese.

(4) Roll out remaining dough for top crust. With a cookie cutter, cut remaining dough into 2-inch circle shapes. Overlap the circles on top of the filling, to make a decorative top crust (kind of like a fish-scale pattern).

(5) Bake the pie at 400° for 30 to 35 minutes. Cut into wedges and serve hot.

A Conversation with the Cook... "Many years ago my (then) husband and I had some dear friends, with whom we exchanged a weekly dinner—one week their house, next week our house, experimenting with our favorite recipes. While the men played an after-dinner game of chess, Barbara and I exchanged our cooking knowledge. Barbara was such an accomplished cook, and I newly married, coveted her wonderful recipes. This is one of those memorable dishes and has long remained a personal favorite of mine. If you don't want to tackle the homemade crust, substitute ready made pie shells, but I must advise you, the fabulous crust is what takes this dish over the top! To make the dish even more intriguing, Barbara used to serve it in a Gold Miner's Pan!—at least that is what she told me."

"In the end, your creativity—perhaps even your outrageousness—will determine the final result."
~Bobby Flay

Oven Roasting Beef 101

Prime Rib:
1. Place roast in pan on ribs, meaty side curved up, and resting on ends of bones.
2. Roast for 20 minutes at 450°.
3. Reduce heat to 350° and continue to roast 10 to 12 minutes more/per pound for medium rare. Serve with warmed "au jus" on the side, or Madeira Sauce recipe that follows.

Whole Filet Mignon:
1. Roast in hot 450° oven for 10 minutes/per pound.
2. Serve sliced with a gourmet sauce and/or sautéed mushrooms.

Sirloin Tip Roast:
1. Roast for 20 minutes at 450°.
2. Turn down oven temperature to 350° and continue roasting for 10 minutes more/per pound.

A Conversation with the Cook... "These temperatures are based on a medium-pink center. If someone prefers more done or well-done, serve them an end-cut; or put their cut back in the oven or under the broiler to finish cooking to their liking. Select the finest cuts of beef you can afford. (I like to use Certified Black Angus.) Serve any of these cuts with the Madeira Sauce that follows, or a pre-made 'au jus' (beef broth) for dipping."

Madeira Sauce to Accompany Roast Beef
Makes approximately 2 cups

1 (10.5 ounce) can beef bouillon
1 tablespoon cornstarch
1/2 cup Madeira wine (can be found at better liquor stores)
2 tablespoons Escoffier Sauce Diable ® (or as a second choice 3 tablespoons Sauce Robert®, or third choice 2 tablespoons Kitchen Bouquet®)—find these at a gourmet store or in the special-foods section of your market)
Fresh sliced mushrooms, sautéed in a little butter
1 tablespoon butter, to "finish" sauce at end of cooking

In a sauce pan, over medium heat, bring bouillon to a simmer. Mix cornstarch and Madeira by shaking in a small lidded jar. Add mixture to bouillon in saucepan and simmer to thicken. Add the Escoffier Sauce Diable® (or similar choice) for flavor. Keep stirring all the while. Toward end of cooking fold in a package of sliced mushrooms that have been lightly sautéed in a little butter. Lastly, swirl in 1 tablespoon of butter until it melts—this "finishes" the sauce with a nice gloss and extra flavor (it's a French thing) to add that extra touch.

A Conversation with the Cook... "It's that attention to detail, specialty flavors, and your personalized care that always turn ho-hum into yum-yum."

Traditional Roast Turkey with Pan Gravy and Stuffing-on-the-Side

Makes 8 to 12 servings, with suggestions for all the trimmings

The Turkey:

An 8 to 12 -pound turkey, thawed (this will take 2 days in fridge)
Note* Select an 8, 10, 12, or maybe even a 14 -pound turkey. Avoid the larger birds, as they take a longer cooking time, have a tendency to dry out, and require more cooking attention.
Olive oil or unsalted butter
Salt and pepper
1 orange, quartered
1 apple, quartered
1 onion, quartered
1 or 2 stalks celery, cut into chunks
1 or 2 bay leaves and/or a sprig of Rosemary (both optional)
Instant-read meat thermometer, for testing doneness
Heavy-duty disposable foil roasting pan (This is a must; be kind to yourself.)

Plan ahead and begin thawing your turkey 2 days in advance, in the refrigerator, in its commercial wrapping. When cooking-day arrives, remove all wrapping; remove giblets (reserving for gravy or stuffing) and any packaging from cavity; rinse the turkey inside and out in cold running water, and pat dry with paper toweling. (Be sure to keep the outer wrapping, as it will have cooking guidelines written right on it to help you.)

Rub outside of turkey with olive oil or unsalted butter. Season the turkey inside and out with salt and pepper. Also season the little neck/breast-cavity and re-fold the skin back into place. Fold wings behind neck. Loosely put the fruit, onion, and celery into the cavity of the bird. Add the bay leaves/and or Rosemary if you wish. Tie ("truss") the legs together with string. (As the turkey bakes, the fruit, vegetables, and spices will add flavoring and moisture into the meat. This mixture is to be discarded later, as it is only used to flavor the meat.)

In case you are wondering where the stuffing is— your favorite family-recipe for stuffing will be cooked in a casserole dish, alongside the bird, the last hour of cooking. Cooking an un-stuffed bird will hasten total cooking time; and baking the stuffing in a casserole (rather than in the cavity of the bird) will make for less-dense stuffing.

Cooking Method #1 / place prepared bird on a greased cooking rack, breast side down. (Or, as a second choice, Cooking Method #2 / place bird in roasting pan breast side up and loosely tent bird with heavy-duty foil.) Roast in a 325° oven until bird reaches a doneness temperature of at least 165° when a meat thermometer is placed in thickest part of thigh, but avoiding the bone.

(You can refer to your cooking times and directions on the packaging for estimated cooking time. Baste the bird every once in a while with more olive oil, or unsalted butter, or the roasting-pan juices, as they develop.)

Once turkey has reached 165° increase your oven temperature to 425°. For Cooking Method #1, flip the turkey over to breast side up and bake for another half hour, browning and basting the bird to a perfect golden brown. (For Cooking Method #2, remove the foil and baste and brown the bird in the same manner.) When meat in the thigh reaches a temperature of 170° to 175° (check again with your meat thermometer) the bird should be done, nicely browned, and meat tender and moist.

Total cooking time will very with size of bird, but a general guide line is: around 3 hours for 8-pound turkey, 4 hours for 12-pound turkey, with a final meat temperature of 170° to 175°.

Remove turkey to a warm serving platter and tent with foil. Let rest 15 to 20 minutes before carving. This will allow the juices to be absorbed back into the meat, preventing a dried-out bird. While turkey rests, make the gravy from drippings collected while cooking.

Traditional Pan Gravy:
Put roasting pan on stove top over medium-high heat. Skim off any fats that are floating on top. In a small jar, shake together 3 tablespoons flour with 3 tablespoons water, to make a smooth mixture. Pour into pan and stir and cook into juices, getting up all bits on bottom of pan. Cook and stir until mixture thickens. Slowly add approximately 2 cups water, or canned chicken broth, stirring (I like to use a wire whisk) constantly until you arrive at desired consistency. Season to taste with salt and pepper.

Serve gravy in a small warm bowl (keeping the rest warm in the pan on the stove top). Re-fill your gravy bowl as needed, and you will always have nice warm gravy.

Preparation of Giblets
(to use in Pan Gravy or in Stuffing):
While turkey is cooking rinse and simmer the giblets (that little package of innards you found in the cavity) in a saucepan of water, for at least an hour; set aside. Chop the giblets fine in a wooden bowl with a sharp-bladed chopper and reserve to add to the gravy. Save the simmered liquid for the gravy also. Using the Pan Gravy Recipe, substitute giblet-juice in place of water or broth, and stir in the chopped giblets to flavor the gravy. If using for Stuffing Recipe, add the chopped giblets to the stuffing and moisten the stuffing with 4 or 5 tablespoons of their cooking-liquid.

A Conversation with the Cooks... "There are as many ways to cook a turkey as there are cooks. By choosing this very basic oven recipe, we hope to have made this holiday tradition a little less daunting for you. If you are feeling a little adventuresome, why not cook the turkey on the grill, in a smoker, or even a deep-fryer-method, or an extra-large, oval crockery-pot! —All of these methods have their own specific directions (usually accompanying the appliance when purchased) and offer wonderful **alternatives** to traditional-oven-roasting. This will free-up your kitchen for all the extra goodies we've suggested to accompany this fine bird! *Note* Like our oven-baked turkey, all of these alternative cooking methods, also call for an* **un-stuffed** *bird.*

The Side-Dish Stuffing:
Make your family-favorite-recipe and place in a buttered casserole dish. Last hour of roasting the bird, place the casserole in the oven, loosely covered with foil and bake alongside the bird. Your stuffing (or also called "dressing") will be perfectly done, light and fluffy, when the bird is done.

Basic Bread Stuffing:
1 stick butter or margarine, melted
1/2 cup diced onion
1 cup diced celery
8 to 10 cups cubed, day old bread
1/2 teaspoon each: salt, pepper, and sage
1 teaspoon poultry seasoning
4 to 5 tablespoons water, chicken broth, or giblet-simmering water

Sauté onion and celery in melted butter until softened. Toss with remaining ingredients to make stuffing. Put in greased casserole dish and cover loosely with foil. Bake alongside turkey for last hour of cooking.

A Conversation with the Cooks... "Just as there are many ways to prepare a turkey, there are equally as many 'family-favorite-recipes' to make dressing. To this basic recipe you can add mushrooms, dried fruits, raisins, Craisins™, wild rice, roasted chestnuts, water chestnuts, toasted almonds, cooked and crumbled sausage, **cooked and chopped giblets**, corn bread, seasoned croutons, along with a variety of spices—hot, mild, spicy, Cajun, French—the list is long and varied according to regional preferences and ethnic backgrounds. Our recipe is meant to be a 'starting point' for you to develop a favorite of your own."

All-the-Trimmings:
Complete your dinner menu with recipes from our other chapters (see suggestions to follow). You'll find breads, salads, vegetable side-dishes, condiments, and desserts to add to your feast—some can be made ahead; some can cook alongside your turkey, and some can be made 'outside the oven' altogether.

Suggested Super Sides from Chapter Six:
 Corn Pudding ... 196
 Betty's Celery Bake Side Dish ... 200
 Koopmann's Favorite Baked Dish ... 209
 Madame's Yams ... 203
 Double Baked Potatoes Parmesan ... 193
 Baked Hot Fruit Compote ... 207
 June's Baked Carrot Mold ... 204

A Sampling from Chapter Seven:
 Frozen Cranberry Cream Mold ... 227
 Surprise Gelatin Mold ... 247
 Fresh Fruit Tray with Frosted Grapes ... 225
 Marshmallow Mint Salad ... 246

Breads from Chapter Eight:
 Lemon Bread ... 260
 Angie's Pumpkin Bread ... 274
 Sweet Potato Biscuits ... 285
 Aunt Emma's Hot Corn Bread ... 267

Something Sweet from Chapter Nine:
Cranberry Apple Pie ... 299
Southern Chess Pie ... 303
Poppy Seed Pound Cake ... 315
Gingerbread-Currant Cakes-in-a-Jar ... 341

A Conversation with the Cooks... "Make plenty of sides to "stretch out" your menu. Hopefully you will have some turkey left over for the next day. There is nothing better than a Turkey Club Sandwich, Mary-Ann's Tetrazzini (see page 94), or one of our many casseroles with the addition of leftover turkey—for an easy meal a day or two later. You can also save the carcass and make soup! 'So there you have it'—the daunting Turkey Dinner, made ever so easy, step by step."

*"One of the very nicest things about life
is the way we must regularly stop
whatever we are doing
and devote our attention to eating."
~Luciano Pavarotti*

Mediterranean Pot Roast
Makes 8 servings

1 (4 pound) beef rump roast
Flour, for dredging
2 tablespoons vegetable oil
2/3 cup pimiento-stuffed green olives, chopped
1/2 cup raisins
2 to 3 cloves garlic, mashed and minced
4 strips bacon
1 large onion, sliced into rings
1 (32 ounce) can whole tomatoes, crushed
1/4 cup Madeira wine
Salt and pepper

Dredge roast on all sides in flour. Brown quickly on all sides in vegetable oil. Cut deep slits into meat on all sides. Mix olives, raisins, and garlic; and stuff into cuts in the meat. Transfer stuffed roast to Dutch oven or roasting pan; lay bacon strips over roast. Arrange onion rings around and over bacon-covered roast. Pour on tomatoes. Pour on wine. Season with salt and pepper to taste. "Tent" meat with foil; then put on pot-cover. Bake at 325° for 2 1/2 hours. Serve hot with pan juices.

A Conversation with the Cook... "'Tenting' meat with a loose covering of foil, before putting on the pot's cover, helps to tenderize the meat by circulating moisture back down into the meat while cooking—a method used to tenderize many lesser cuts of meat."

Peach-Stuffed Chicken Breasts
Makes 6 servings

Chicken:
6 boneless, skinless, chicken breast halves, *butterflied and *pounded thin (see conversation with the cook)
1/2 teaspoon salt
3 fresh peaches, pitted, peeled, and chopped
1/2 cup onion, chopped fine
1/2 cup cashews, chopped
1/2 teaspoon powdered ginger
1/2 cup butter, melted
1 recipe Fresh Peach Sauce

Slice each chicken breast in half lengthwise, and spread out like a "butterfly." Pound each to flatten (pieces will literally become heart shaped) and sprinkle with the salt. Set aside. Make filling of peaches, peeled and cut into small pieces, onion, cashews, and ginger. Place 1/6 filling on each piece of chicken, roll-up and secure with toothpicks. Pour melted butter over bottom of foil-lined baking pan and place stuffed chicken breasts on the butter. Bake at 350° for 25 minutes, turn chicken over and bake 20 minutes longer. Serve with Fresh Peach Sauce:

Fresh Peach Sauce:
2 fresh peaches, pitted, peeled, and sliced
1/2 cup brown sugar
2 teaspoons prepared mustard
1/4 teaspoon salt
1 cup sour cream

1 tablespoon Brandy

Combine fresh peaches, with brown sugar, mustard, salt, sour cream, and Brandy. Heat for 5 minutes in a saucepan—but do not boil. Serve warm with the peach-filled chicken breasts.

A Conversation with the Cook... "To *butterfly a chicken breast, carefully slice (horizontally) through the middle of the breast, stopping before you actually cut it in half. Fold the meat open, so it looks like a butterfly. To *pound thin, place between 2 sheets of waxed paper and pound with a mallet or the back of a wooden spoon, to flatten, spread, and thin the chicken until you arrive at the thickness and size desired (and by the way this is a great stress-releaser). Your chicken is now ready to continue with recipe."

"I feel a recipe is only a theme, which an intelligent cook can play each time with a variation."
~Madam Benoit

Red Snapper with Garden Sauce

Makes 4 to 6 servings

1 to 1 1/2 pounds Red Snapper fillets
2 tablespoons olive oil
1/2 cup each: chopped onion, chopped green pepper, and chopped celery
1/4 cup carrot, sliced
1 clove garlic, peeled and crushed
1 sprig parsley
1 (15 ounce) can tomato sauce with tomato bits
1/2 cup dry Sherry
1 teaspoon dill weed
1/2 teaspoon each: salt and black pepper
1 tablespoon lemon juice
Lemon slices, for garnish

Thaw fish if frozen. Cut fillets into four to six portions. To make garden sauce, combine olive oil, onion, celery, green pepper, carrot, parsley, and garlic in saucepan. Cover and cook until vegetables are tender, 5 to 7 minutes. Stir in tomato sauce, Sherry, and dill. Bring to boil, then gently simmer 10 minutes. Place about 1/2 cup sauce-mixture in bottom of 12 x 8-inch baking dish. Place fish portions over sauce and sprinkle with salt, pepper, and the lemon juice. Pour remaining sauce over fish. Bake at 400° 15 to 20 minutes, or until fish flakes easily when tested with fork.

A Conversation with the Cook..."The next time your husband comes home with fresh-caught Walleye, put away the frying pan and try this recipe!"

Roast Cornish Hens
Makes 12 servings, at 1/2 hen per person

6 Rock Cornish hens, split in half
1 1/2 cups flour
3 teaspoons salt
1 teaspoon black pepper
1 1/2 cups shortening (I use half butter, half shortening)
Melted butter
Paprika

Rinse hens and pat dry. Cut in half with a kitchen shears. Mix flour, salt, and pepper; coat hens with flour mixture. In oven, melt shortening-mixture in two baking pans, each 13 x 9 x 2-inches. Place hens skin-side down in melted shortening. Bake uncovered 45 minutes in 425° oven. Turn hens over and bake 15 minutes longer. Brush with additional melted butter and sprinkle with paprika for beautiful color. Serve with mashed potatoes, a vegetable side dish, and our *Bonus Recipe*, Never Fail Wild Rice.

A Conversation with the Cook... "Cornish hens make such a fancy dinner and are so easy. *Bonus Recipe:* While hens are baking, prepare a **Never Fail Wild Rice Side Dish**. In a large pot gently boil for 45 minutes, 1 cup wild rice in 4 cups water (always use a ratio of 1 part rice to 4 parts water and always use a deep pot as the mixture tends to 'foam up'). The grain will begin to soften and pop. Drain off any remaining water and wrap the hot rice in a tea towel and place wrapped rice in a colander. Place the colander onto a deep pot that has 1 or 2-inches of boiling water in it (in essence you are creating a double boiler or steamer). Cover tightly with foil. Steam the rice, covered, for 15 to 20 minutes more until the rice is puffy and tender. To serve, un-wrap and transfer to a warm serving dish, fold in sautéed mushrooms, a little salt and pepper to taste, and drizzle with melted butter. The nice thing about this cooking method is that you can 'hold' the rice quite a while during the steaming process, if you find your dinner is not yet done. Expensive, but worth every penny, Wild Rice makes a fabulous side dish to any meal, especially Cornish Game Hens or Wild Game."

Stuffed Crown Roast of Pork
Makes 12 servings for a **very** festive occasion

6 to 8-pound pork crown roast with ribs *Note:* be sure to pre-order from your butcher and have him trim and tie the roast for you ahead of time.
1 teaspoon salt
1 teaspoon pepper
8 cups bread stuffing (use your favorite)
Fancy "paper booties" at serving time (optional)

Season meat with salt and pepper. Stand roast bone-end tips up in open shallow roasting pan; wrap bone-end tips in aluminum foil to prevent excessive browning. To hold shape of roast, rest a small oven-proof bowl or cup in the crown. Insert meat thermometer so tip is in thickest part of meat and does not rest on fat or bone. Do not add water. Do not cover. Roast in a 325° oven, 30 to 35 minutes per pound or until meat thermometer registers 170°. One hour before meat is done, remove bowl from center of crown; fill crown with your choice of bread stuffing. Cover just the stuffing with aluminum foil during first 30 minutes, then remove last half hour. When roast is done, remove foil from protected bone-end tips and replace with optional "paper booties" (you can find these in gourmet shops) when you are ready to serve. Place roast on serving platter, up-right like a "crown." To carve, remove stuffing to serving bowl; cut roast between ribs. Each serving should include a rib. Serve with a selected choice of side dishes for a regal feast fit for a king's gathering.

A Conversation with the Cook... "Optional: garnish stuffing with sliced water chestnuts, or sliced toasted almonds (see suggested ways to toast nuts on page 40). Garnish serving platter with spiced peaches and/or spiced crab apples, or apple rings. Serve as a very special dinner for a special occasion. Let the head of the household carve and serve."

"A Recipe for Happiness"
3 heaping cups of patience
1 heart full of love
2 handfuls of generosity
Dash of laughter
Handful of understanding
Combine ingredients. Sprinkle with kindness. Add plenty of faith. Mix well.
Spread over a lifetime. Serve everyone.
~Kitchen Proverb

My Pork Chops with Tomato-Olive Sauce
Makes 6 servings

6 thick-cut pork chops
1/4 cup green olives with pimentos, sliced
4 medium-size fresh tomatoes
1 tablespoon olive oil
1 tablespoon flour
1/2 teaspoon salt
1/2 teaspoon pepper

Trim fat from chops; sprinkle both sides with salt. Heat oil in pan and brown both sides of chops (10 to 15 minutes). Reserve at least 2 tablespoons of pan drippings. Meanwhile, place peeled, sliced tomatoes and green olives in bottom of shallow 13 x 9-inch casserole. Combine flour, salt, and pepper; sprinkle over tomatoes and olives. Place browned chops on top of tomato-mixture. Measure 2 tablespoons drippings from pan and pour over chops. Cover and bake at 375° for 1 hour.

A Conversation with the Cook... "I'm going to let you in on a little secret ... Tomatoes, when added to roasts will help to naturally tenderize them. Tomatoes contain an acid that works to break down meat, making them one of Nature's automatic tenderizers. This works especially well with pork chops, and lesser cuts of meat, making them very tender, while keeping them moist as well."

Grandma Scherer's Baked Tenderloin

Makes 6 servings

1 whole beef tenderloin
2 tablespoons butter
1/2 cup green onion, chopped
1 teaspoon dry mustard
3/4 cup red burgundy wine
2 tablespoons soy sauce

Combine butter, green onion, dry mustard, wine, and soy sauce; heat in saucepan. Place tenderloin in baking pan; pour heated mixture over top. Bake 20 minutes at 400°; then increase temperature to 425° for 15 minutes more. Cut into individual portions. Serve with Double Baked Potatoes Parmesan (page 193) and Grilled Garden Tomatoes (page 234).

A Conversation with the Cook... "Whenever possible, carve meat across the grain. Meat will be easier to eat and have a better appearance when served."

Suzanne's Glazed Pork Tenderloin

Makes 4 servings

1 orange
1/4 cup soy sauce
1 teaspoon fresh minced ginger
Salt and pepper to taste
1 pound pork tenderloin

Grate 1 teaspoon of the colored zest from the orange and squeeze 1/4 cup of the juice. Combine the zest, juice, soy sauce, and ginger in a sauce pan. Boil until liquid is reduced to about 2 tablespoons, about 3 to 4 minutes. Place tenderloin in shallow baking dish and brush glaze over the pork. Season with salt and pepper to taste. Roast in 325° oven until cooked through, about 40 minutes, or test with meat thermometer for doneness.

A Conversation with the Cook... "Zest is the outer rind of citrus fruit (lemons, limes, oranges, etc.) that contains the fruit's flavor-perfume, also known as 'essence.' The outer rind can be of varying thickness and graininess and can have either a bumpy or a smooth texture. Cold fruits with a thick, bumpy texture yield the most zest. When you are grating zest, be careful to get only the colored rind, not the white-ish pulp underneath, which is very bitter."

Chicken Bake No Peek

Makes 5 to 6 servings

1 1/2 cups uncooked rice
1 can mushroom soup
1 can cream of chicken soup
1 soup can full of water
1 package dry onion soup mix
5 to 6 boneless, skinless chicken breast halves
Salt and pepper to taste

Mix rice, soups, salt, pepper, and water; put into 13 x 9-inch pan. Top with chicken breasts. Sprinkle with dry onion soup mix. Cover securely with foil and bake 2 1/2 hours at 350°. DO NOT PEEK or rice will not cook properly.

A Conversation with the Cook... "Keep the foil on tight until the dish is done and your chicken is going to be oh so tender and the rice oh so perfectly fluffy— trust me."

"Cooking is a little like religion.
Have faith in the process and trust
your instructions."
~MaryAnn

New Orleans-Style Chicken

Makes 4 servings

4 boneless, skinless chicken breast halves
4 tablespoons melted butter, divided
6 tablespoons flour
3/4 teaspoon salt
1/2 teaspoon pepper
1/4 teaspoon sweet Hungarian paprika
3/4 cup white wine or water
1 teaspoon chicken bouillon crystals or 1 cube
1/4 teaspoon poultry seasoning
1 bay leaf
1 3/4 cups sliced mushrooms
1/2 cup onion, sliced
3/4 cup celery, chopped
1/2 cups carrots, grated
3/4 cup sour cream
Cooked white or brown rice, at serving time

Mix flour, salt, pepper, and paprika in a shallow pan. Roll chicken breasts in flour mixture to coat. Save leftover mixture. Place chicken breasts in large frying pan with 2 tablespoons melted butter and brown lightly on both sides. Remove chicken from frying pan and reserve. In a 13 x 9-inch baking dish mix wine, leftover flour mixture, and remaining 2 tablespoons melted butter. Whisk to blend. Add all seasonings and vegetables. Place reserved chicken breasts on top. Bake at 350° for 30 minutes. Remove chicken to a serving platter and remove bay leaf from sauce. Add sour cream to mixture in baking dish. Stir to blend and pour sauce over chicken. Serve with rice.

A Conversation with the Cook... "—a little taste of Creole from a Mid-western kitchen."

Glenn's Stuffed Pork Chops
Makes 6 servings

6 pork chops, 1-inch thick
4 tablespoons shortening, divided
2 tablespoon green pepper, chopped fine
2 tablespoons celery, chopped fine
6 tablespoons onion, chopped fine
1 teaspoon salt
2 cups stuffing-style bread crumbs
1/2 cup evaporated milk
Water, as needed

Split the chops through the center to the bone, making a pocket to hold stuffing. Melt half the shortening in frying pan, add the onion until delicately browned, add green pepper, celery, salt, and bread crumbs. Moisten with milk and mix to make stuffing. Fill the chops, each with 1/6 stuffing and fasten with skewers or tie with cord. Place in roaster pan and season with additional salt and pepper. Brown the rest of the shortening in original frying pan and pour over chops. Cover the bottom of chop-filled roaster pan with water. Bake chops at 400° about 1 hour, or until tender and cooked through. Turn chops over half-way through cooking. Serve with Homemade Applesauce (see page 215) and Corn Pudding Side Dish (see page 196).

A Conversation with the Cook... "Picture-perfect pork chops that taste as good as they look ... bring a hearty appetite to the table."

Hawaiian Spareribs

Makes 6 servings

4 pounds spareribs (use baby back ribs)
1 cup brown sugar, packed
1 teaspoon salt
2 tablespoon cornstarch
1/2 cup water
2 tablespoons Worcestershire sauce
1/3 cup wine vinegar
1/4 cup soy sauce
1 teaspoon ground ginger
1 teaspoon orange rind
1/4 cup onion, minced
4 dashes Tabasco sauce
1 (8 ounce) can crushed pineapple (do not drain)

Place ribs, meaty side up, in an 18 x 13 x 1 3/4-inch Pyrex® dish. Mix all remaining ingredients together and pour over ribs, coating well. Cover and let ribs marinate all day or overnight in refrigerator. Remove covering and bake at 375° for 1 hour. Remove any rendered grease from pan juices and discard. Brush sauce over ribs again and bake for at least 30 minutes more, or until meat is tender-falling-off-the-bone and well-glazed.

A Conversation with the Cook... "Sweet and succulent, this is a great way to enjoy ribs."

Mary's Roast Rib-Eye
Makes 4 to 6 servings

1 tablespoon oil
1 (4 pound) rib-eye roast
1 Spanish onion, peeled and diced
2 garlic gloves, peeled
1/2 teaspoon thyme
3/4 teaspoon crushed oregano
1/2 teaspoon dried basil
1 bay leaf
1 tablespoon chopped parsley
1 cup dry red wine
1 (28 ounce) can tomatoes and juice
3 tablespoons tomato paste
Salt
Pepper
Tabasco sauce, few drops

Heat oil in very large oven-proof casserole. Add meat and "sear" 7 to 8 minutes over high heat to seal in juices. Turn meat to brown all sides and season well with salt and pepper. Add onion, garlic, and herbs; mix well. Cook 7 to 8 minutes more over medium-high heat. Pour in tomatoes with juice and mix again. Season well with salt and pepper to taste and add tomato paste, then Tabasco sauce. Bring pan sauces to a boil. Put cover on casserole and transfer to 350° oven. Bake roast for 3 hours, or until meat is very tender.

A Conversation with the Cook... "A Dutch oven works perfectly for this recipe and the following one. I like to use a pot that can cook on the stove top and then in the oven—makes clean-up a breeze, as you have only one dish!"

Braised Rib-Eye Steaks
Makes 4 servings

1 1/2 tablespoons oil
2 rib-eye steaks, fat trimmed
Salt and pepper to taste
1 large Spanish onion, peeled and diced large
1 teaspoon dried oregano
1 garlic clove, smashed and chopped
2 celery stalks, diced large
3 tomatoes, cut in wedges
1 tablespoon chopped parsley
1 cup tomato-clam juice
2 cups hot beef stock
1 medium-size turnip, peeled and cubed

Heat oil in large sauté pan. When hot, add meat and sear 2 to 3 minutes each side. Season well with salt and pepper. Add onion and oregano; cook 5 to 6 minutes over medium heat. Mix in garlic, celery, and tomatoes. Turn meat over and add parsley, salt, and pepper. Continue cooking 5 to 6 minutes. Add tomato-clam juice and beef stock. Season well again with salt and pepper to taste. Mix in turnip; bring to boil. Cover pan and transfer to oven; cook 2 hours in 350° oven. When cooked, remove and slice meat (against the grain). Serve slices smothered in pan juices.

A Conversation with the Cook... "To 'braise' means long, slow, covered, moist cooking to tenderize and infuse flavor, usually to a tougher cut of meat. To 'sear' is the first step you do (before you begin braising) by cooking quickly and briefly over high heat, to initially brown the meat on all sides and seal in its moisture, so that it will remain succulent during the following cooking. A French touch for braising is to 'tent' (or double cover) the meat, by first loosely covering the meat with a layer of foil and then putting the cover on the pot. This double-covering helps direct all the moisture back down into the meat while it's braising. Again use your Dutch oven, or a similar pot that works well on both stovetop and in oven—for one pot cooking."

Chapter Five
"The Top Twenty" ...
Twenty of Our Favorite Casseroles

✧

*"Ask not what you can do for your country.
Ask what's for lunch."
~Orson Welles*

Recipe Index

Cazuela de Quesa y Championes (Casserole of Baked Cheese and Mushrooms) ... 163
Suzi's Mexican Vegetarian Casserole ... 165
Seafood Medley ... 166
Seafood N Biscuits Cobbler ... 168
Mediterranean Zucchini Bake ... 169
Casserole Beef Stew ... 170
Shrimp d' Jonghe ... 171
Annabelle's Tuna Casserole ... 172
Sammy's Wieneroni Casserole ... 173
Suzanne's Garden Supper Dish ... 174
Great Spaghetti Bake ... 175
Grandma Scherer's Baked Stuffed Shells ... 177
Round Steak N Ravioli ... 180

Pizza Pop-Up Casserole ... 181
Beef Noodle Casserole ... 183
Angel's Beef and Potato Bake ... 184
Angie's Hot Chicken Salad ... 185
Angie's Seafood Hot Dish ... 186
Easy and Good Beef and Biscuits ... 187
Pork Casserole ... 188

Cazuela de Quesa y Championes (Casserole of Baked Cheese and Mushrooms)

Flexible recipe—make as much or as little as you want.

(1) In a buttered shallow cazuela (casserole dish) layer the following:
Sliced mushrooms (topped with)
Chopped onion (topped with)
Shredded or diced Monterey Jack cheese (topped with)
Shredded or diced Cheddar cheese

(2) Season this mixture (to taste) with liberal shakes of: Garlic powder, Sea salt, Cayenne, Cumin, Chili powder, Crushed cilantro and just a slight pinch of Cinnamon.

(3) Repeat another layer of mushrooms, onion, and cheeses—then more seasonings. End with a little more plain cheese over the very top.

(4) You will need Soft Flour Tortillas, at time of serving.

(5) Bake assembled casserole in 400° oven until all is bubbly, melted, blended, and ooey-gooey. Serve spoonfuls of the baked cheese wrapped in soft, warmed flour tortillas, kept warm in a napkin-lined basket.

A Conversation with the Cook... "I became addicted to this dish, after first experiencing it in a little-sidewalk restaurant in the Zona Rosa of Mexico City. There it was served along side a "barbecoa" of grilled meats that took center stage. When I got home, I was having 'cazuela de quesa' withdrawal, so I devised my own version. Wrapped in warm tortillas, this cheese dish makes a wonderful light dinner or satisfying snack. Kids love it too—after they 'pick out' the mushrooms."

Suzi's Mexican Vegetarian Casserole

Makes 6 to 8 servings

Casserole:
1 (15 ounce) can whole kernel corn, drained
1 (15 ounce) can black beans, rinsed and drained
1 (10 ounce) can tomatoes with green chilies
1 (8 ounce) container sour cream
1 (8 ounce) jar Picante sauce
2 cups shredded mild Cheddar cheese
2 to 3 cups cooked rice
1/4 teaspoon pepper

Topping:
1 small bunch green onions, chopped to include tops
1 smallish to medium can sliced black olives, drained
1 (8 ounce) package Monterey Jack shredded cheese

Combine first 8 ingredients and spoon into lightly greased 9 x 13-inch baking dish. Top with green onions, sliced black olives, and shredded Monterey Jack cheese. Bake at 350° for 50 to 60 minutes. Serve warm, with additional sour cream as a garnish.

Note: this dish may also be served with the addition of a pound of ground beef, sautéed very well, drained of fat, and crumbled very fine. Mix the sautéed meat into the vegetarian bean/rice mixture to make and even tastier dish now suitable for meat lovers. Continue with recipe as written.

A Conversation with the Cook... "This is absolutely a fabulous dish that has 'made the rounds' from Suzi's office (in our apartment complex) to my kitchen! Last year when a friend threw me a birthday dinner, she asked what I would like her to make, and without hesitation, I responded Suzi's Mexican Casserole! I love it vegetarian style (as a side dish along with a meat entrée) and I love it with the meat added (turning it into a main-dish entrée)—both are delicious and make easy recipes for the beginner cook."

✧

Seafood Medley
Makes 4 to 6 rich servings

Sauce:
2 tablespoons melted butter
1/4 cup flour
2 cups half-and-half
1 teaspoon salt
1/4 cup Sherry
1/2 teaspoon MSG (optional, I tend not to use it)
1/4 teaspoon white pepper

Sea food:
1/2 pound sautéed scallops
1/2 pound cooked lobster meat
1/2 pound cooked crab meat
1/2 pound cooked shrimp

Other stuff:
1/2 pound sliced mushrooms sautéed
1/3 cup grated Parmesan cheese
1/4 cup dry bread crumbs
Butter

In saucepan, over medium heat, make a white sauce by combining butter and flour to make a roux. Stir in half-and-half and remaining ingredients, cooking and stirring to thicken; reserve. To assemble, spread 1/3 cup sauce in buttered au gratin dish. Arrange sea foods in layers into the dish, moistening each layer with more sauce as you go. Top with the sautéed mushrooms and drizzle with remaining sauce. Mix together Parmesan and bread crumbs and sprinkle over all as a topping. Dot with butter. Bake at 350° for 30 to 45 minutes, or until all is bubbly, heated through, and topping is golden brown.

A Conversation with the Cook... "Not for the faint of heart or the faint of budget, I reserve this dish for special occasions. You'll notice throughout this book I use a lot of white pepper in my fancier recipes. It is great to use in creamy dishes and those with white sauces, so you don't have 'little black specs' in your food."

Sea Food N Biscuits Cobbler
Makes 4+ servings

1 (10.5 ounce) can cream of mushroom soup, undiluted
1/4 cup Sherry
1/2 cup half-and-half cream
1 (7.75 ounce) can crabmeat, drained
1 (4.5 ounce) can shrimp, drained
1/4 cup slivered almonds
1 cup shredded Swiss cheese
1 tube Pillsbury® Buttermilk Biscuits
Chopped fresh chives

Heat first 6 ingredients together until bubbly. Stir in the cheese until it melts. Pour into un-greased 2 - quart casserole dish. Separate biscuits and place on top. Garnish with chopped chives. Bake at 400° for 20 minutes, or until biscuits are well browned. Scoop out servings to include biscuits in each.

A Conversation with the Cook... "Sea food and Sherry ... a match made in heaven. If you do not elect to keep a drinkable Sherry on hand, a cooking Sherry, found in the gourmet-condiment aisle of your market, will do just fine in the recipe."

*"Fish, to taste right, must swim three times—
in water, in butter, in wine."
~Polish Proverb*

Mediterranean Zucchini Bake
Makes 6 to 8 servings

1 1/2 pounds lamb/veal/beef mixture
1 cup chopped leek (If you are not familiar with leeks ask your fresh produce manager to show you one. They look like gigantic green onions, but paler and have a mild onion-y taste.)
1 clove garlic, mashed and minced
1/2 teaspoon fines herbs
1/2 teaspoon salt
Dash of cinnamon
1 (10 ounce) package frozen spinach, thawed, moisture drained and pressed out
6 ounces mozzarella, shredded
2 cups thinly-sliced zucchini rounds
Butter
1/3 cup Parmesan cheese

Sauté ground meats with leek and garlic. Add spices. Fold in spinach, then cheese. Put mixture in 9 x 13 - inch baking dish. Arrange 2 cups of thinly sliced zucchini rounds on top, in lengthwise rows. Dot with butter, sprinkle with 1/3 cup Parmesan cheese. Bake at 350° for 45 minutes.

A Conversation with the Cook... "Surprisingly enough, just a slight dash of cinnamon lends great authentic flavor and aroma to Mexican, Spanish, and Mediterranean foods. It is a secret to many of my ethnic recipes. Use sparingly—you want just an unidentifiable hint!"

Casserole Beef Stew
Makes 6 servings

2 pounds stew meat; don't brown
4 to 5 carrots
3 onions, chopped
1 cup chopped celery
5 potatoes, scrubbed, peeled and halved
1 tablespoon sugar
2 tablespoons dry cornstarch
Salt and pepper to taste
1 1/2 cups tomato juice

Put first 5 ingredients in order given in casserole dish that has a tight fitting cover. Mix sugar and dry cornstarch; sprinkle over vegetables. Season lightly with salt and pepper. Add tomato juice. Cover and bake at 300° for 4 hours. Serve straight from the pot.

A Conversation with the Cook... "A lot of bang for your buck, this recipe is easy on the pocket book, while serving up great old-fashioned flavor with the use of **a lot** of onion. The long, slow cooking is perfect for a winter day and is a standard favorite for our top twenty."

"I will not move my army without onions."
~ Ulysses S. Grant, U. S. General

Shrimp d' Jonghe

Makes 6 individual casseroles, at 6 to 8 shrimp per casserole

Approximately 3 pounds uncooked large shrimp, cleaned, deveined, tails removed (you need 6 to 8 per casserole)
Salt and pepper to taste
1/2 cup consommé or white wine
6 cloves garlic, smashed but not chopped
1 cup butter
2 cups dry bread crumbs
6 tablespoons minced fresh parsley
1 tablespoon Sherry, or cooking Sherry
Lemon wedges, at serving time

Divide shrimp into 6 buttered individual baking dishes, also known as ramekins. Season with salt and pepper. Drizzle consommé or wine over shrimp. In a sauce pan, cook garlic in butter until butter just begins to bubble and very slightly brown. Immediately remove garlic; add breadcrumbs and parsley to the butter to mix. Distribute crumb mixture over each ramekin. Sprinkle a few drops Sherry on each. Place ramekins in oven and bake for 15 minutes at 400°, or until shrimp are opaque. Do NOT over cook! Place each ramekin on a charger-plate and serve hot and bubbly. Pass lemon wedges.

A Conversation with the Cook... "You could bake-up this dish in a larger shallow casserole, but I think it more fun to serve individual casseroles, or even invest in special shrimp d' jonghe ramekins."

Annabelle's Tuna Casserole
Makes 6 to 8 servings

2 cups uncooked macaroni
1 1/2 cups celery, chopped fine
1/2 cup green pepper, ribbed, seeded, and chopped
1/2 cup onion, chopped
1/4 cup butter
1 (10.75 ounce) can cream of mushroom soup
1 (10.75 ounce) can cream of celery soup
2/3 cup milk
2 cups Cheddar cheese, shredded
1 (12.5 ounce) can tuna
4 ounces pimiento, drained and diced
1/2 teaspoon salt
1/4 teaspoon nutmeg
1/2 cup toasted almonds (optional)

Cook macaroni; drain; set aside. Sauté celery, green pepper, and onion in butter till tender. Add soup, milk, and cheese. Stir till cheese melts. Combine cooked macaroni, cheese mixture, tuna, pimiento, salt, and nutmeg. Pour into 2 1/2-quart casserole dish. Top with almonds. Bake at 350° for 30 to 35 minutes.

A Conversation with the Cook... "Not only does pimiento add a subtle flavor to the dish, it adds color. The hint of nutmeg is key to this dish. I like to grate my nutmeg fresh, on a little grater made just for that purpose."

Sammy's Wieneroni Casserole
Makes 6 servings

1/2 pound bacon, diced
1/2 cup chopped onion
4 teaspoons Worcestershire sauce
1 cup dark corn syrup
3/4 teaspoon salt
1/4 teaspoon paprika
1/3 cup lemon juice
1/2 cup water
1 1/2 cups chili sauce
1 pound wieners
2 tablespoons water
1 tablespoon cornstarch
Cooked Macaroni, at serving time

Fry bacon and onion until bacon is crisp and onion is soft. Drain off fat. Stir in Worcestershire sauce, syrup, salt, paprika, lemon juice, 1/2 cup water, and chili sauce. Bring to a boil. Reduce heat. Blend 2 tablespoons water and cornstarch. Stir into sauce. Stir and boil 1 minute to thicken. Pour sauce into a casserole dish and add wieners. Bake at 350° for 20 minutes. Serve over cooked macaroni.

A Conversation with the Cook... "If you are looking for a different way to serve hotdogs, and macaroni, this is it. Kid friendly, but adults like it too."

"Sweet..."
~Samantha Noel

Suzanne's Garden Supper Dish

Makes 4 servings

2 cups cubed soft bread
3/4 cup shredded Cheddar cheese
2 tablespoons butter, melted
1 cup cooked garden peas
2 tablespoons onion, chopped
3 tablespoons additional butter
3 tablespoons flour
1 teaspoon salt
1/2 teaspoon pepper
1 1/2 cups milk
1 cup cut-up cooked meat (your choice)
1 large garden tomato, sliced

Mix bread cubes, cheese and melted butter. Spread half the mixture in greased 1-quart casserole and top with peas; set aside. Cook and stir onion in 3 tablespoons additional butter until onion is tender. Blend in flour and seasonings. Cook over low heat, stirring until mixture is bubbly. Remove from heat. Stir in milk; return to stove and heat to simmering, stirring constantly. Cook and stir 1 minute, until thickened and smooth. Stir in meat; pour over peas in casserole dish. Arrange tomato slices on top and sprinkle with remaining bread mixture. Bake uncovered 25 minutes at 350° until all is hot and bubbly.

A Conversation with the Cook... "Stop, look, and save those leftovers. Leftovers and a limited budget have inspired many a tasty casserole!"

Great Spaghetti Bake

Makes 8 servings

1 (2 pound) box spaghetti, ready cut noodles
1 1/2 pounds mozzarella cheese
1 (30 ounce) can tomato sauce
2 1/2 tablespoons tomato paste
1/2 cup green pepper, ribbed, seeded, and chopped
1/2 cup onion, chopped
1/2 teaspoon garlic powder
1/2 teaspoon crushed rosemary
2 teaspoons dried oregano
1 teaspoon dried basil
3 teaspoons molasses
3 teaspoon olive oil
1 teaspoon onion powder
1 1/2 teaspoons Italian seasoning

Mix all ingredients (except noodles and cheese); let simmer for at least 2 hours. Prepare noodles (do not overcook). Layer noodles in a 13 x 9-inch baking dish 1/2 to 1-inch from the top. Pour entire sauce mixture on top; cover with mozzarella cheese. Bake at 375° uncovered, until cheese melts. Let set 5 minutes before serving.

A Conversation with the Cook... "This dish smells wonderful when baking...the rosemary, oregano, and basil are all very aromatic herbs. If you have an herb garden, use fresh instead for a wonderful treat! Just double the amount of herbs used."

"All you see, I owe to spaghetti."
~Sophia Loren

Grandma Scherer's Baked Stuffed Shells

Makes 12 servings

1 large onion, peeled and chopped
2 cloves garlic, peeled and chopped
3 tablespoons olive oil
2 (28 ounce) cans whole tomatoes, crushed
1 (12 ounce) can tomato paste
1 teaspoon dried leaf oregano
1/2 teaspoon ground sage
1/2 teaspoon ground cloves
1/2 teaspoon salt
1/2 teaspoon sugar
1 teaspoon Accent®
2 pounds cottage cheese, creamed to smooth
2 eggs, slightly beaten
1 (10 ounce) package frozen chopped spinach, cooked and drained very well
1 cup Parmesan cheese
1 (12 ounce) package large pasta shells
1 (4 ounce) package shredded mozzarella cheese

Sauté onions and garlic in oil in large saucepan until tender. Be careful not to burn garlic, as it will turn bitter. Add tomatoes, tomato paste, oregano, sage, cloves, salt, sugar, and one-half teaspoon Accent®. Bring to boil; lower heat and simmer 60 to 90 minutes, stirring occasionally.

In mixing bowl, mix cottage cheese (that you have creamed to smooth, with the back of a spoon, or a mixer) eggs, spinach, Parmesan cheese, and remaining Accent®. Cook shells according to package directions, not cooking until completely done because they will cook further in casserole. Drain well and fill each shell with cheese mixture.

Spoon one-third of slow-simmered sauce in bottom of very large baking pan. Arrange filled shells on top of sauce. Cover with remaining sauce and sprinkle top with mozzarella cheese. Cover with foil and bake 45 minutes in 375° oven. Remove foil and bake 15 minutes longer.

A Conversation with the Cook... "This dish can be made in advance, refrigerated, and brought to room temperature before baking. Sauce will look as if it has separated when casserole comes out of oven, but let it sit 10 minutes and the sauce will look fine."

A Special Note from MaryAnn... "Grandma Sherer was Italian as Italian could be, with just a hint of Irish mixed in for good measure, and could she cook! I have included several of her 'heirloom recipes' in this book because they are so special. Of course you can substitute many of today's ready-made ingredients (such as your favorite brand spaghetti sauce, already made) but the result will not be quite the same as Grandma Sherer's lovingly tended dish. So on a winter Saturday or Sunday afternoon, gather a girl friend for an afternoon of cooking, and mix up a batch for the both of you ... the old fashioned way ... with the flavor of time and old-fashioned goodness. Your families will be glad you did. If your family is small—divide the dish into 2 casseroles. Eat one tonight and freeze the other for later."

"A pause to say grace increases the appetite."
~MaryAnn

Round Steak N Ravioli

Makes 6 hearty servings

1 1/2 pounds beef round steak, 1 1/2-inches thick
3 tablespoons flour
1/2 teaspoon salt
1/2 teaspoon dried oregano
1/2 teaspoon pepper
1 tablespoon shortening
1 (15.5 ounce) can spaghetti sauce with mushrooms
3 medium zucchini
1 (16 ounce) can tiny whole onions, drained
1 (15.5 ounce) can cheese ravioli in sauce

To start, mix flour and seasonings. Coat meat with flour mixture; reserve remaining flour mixture. Melt shortening in skillet; brown dredged meat. Place in un-greased baking dish, 11 ½ x 7 ½ x 1 ½-inches. Pour spaghetti sauce into skillet; stir in reserved flour mixture. Heat to boiling, stirring constantly. Pour over meat in casserole; cover with aluminum foil. Bake 45 minutes in 375° oven. Meanwhile, cut each zucchini lengthwise in half. Remove casserole from oven and place zucchini and onions in sauce around meat. Spoon ravioli over meat. Cover again with foil; return to oven; bake 45 minutes longer or until meat is tender.

A Conversation with the Cook... "This glorious casserole is a meal in one. It needs only a crisp green salad with your favorite dressing."

Pizza Pop-Up Casserole
Makes 6 servings

1 1/2 pounds ground beef
1 cup onion, chopped
1 cup green pepper, chopped
1 clove garlic
1 teaspoon dried oregano
1/2 cup water
1/8 teaspoon Tabasco sauce
1 (15 ounce) can tomato sauce
1 envelope spaghetti sauce
8 ounces sliced mozzarella cheese
3/4 cup grated Parmesan cheese
1 cup milk
1 tablespoon olive oil
2 eggs
1 cup flour
1/2 teaspoon salt
1/2 teaspoon pepper

Brown meat; drain. Add onion, green pepper, garlic, oregano, pepper, water, Tabasco, tomato sauce, and spaghetti sauce; mix and simmer for 10 minutes. Meanwhile, in small bowl, combine milk, oil, and eggs; beat for 1 minute at medium speed. Add reserved flour and salt; beat another 2 minutes or until smooth; set batter aside. Pour hot meat mixture into ungreased 13 x 9-inch pan. Top with cheese slices. Pour reserved batter over cheese, completely covering the top. Sprinkle with Parmesan cheese and bake for 25 to 30 minutes at 400° or until puffy and golden.

A Conversation with the Cook... "Go ahead and add other vegetables such as mushrooms, zucchini, and black olives to this 'deep-dish' extravaganza."

Beef Noodle Casserole

Makes 6 servings

1 pound ground beef
1 large onion, chopped
4 tablespoons dried sweet peppers
2/3 cup Cheddar cheese
1 (8 ounce) package noodles, cooked and drained
1/2 teaspoon celery salt
1/2 teaspoon Lawry's® seasoned salt
1/2 teaspoon Accent®
1/4 teaspoon chili powder
1 (10.75 ounce) can tomato soup
1 sleeve white crackers, crushed
1 to 2 tablespoons melted butter

Brown ground beef in skillet; add onion and peppers. Add seasonings: celery salt, seasoned salt, Accent®, and chili powder. Taste a few times to test seasoning. Add soup and 1/2 soup-can water and Cheddar cheese to meat mixture. Cook until cheese melts. Spread cooked noodles into large casserole dish and pour meat/cheese mixture over. For topping, crush crackers and toss lightly with melted butter. Put on top of casserole before baking. Bake at 325° for 1 hour.

A Conversation with the Cook... "When adding seasonings add them slowly and taste often to get the flavor you enjoy. Feel free to cut back on some or add more according to your taste."

Angel's Beef and Potato Bake

Makes 6 to 8 servings

1 teaspoon oil
2 onions, peeled and finely chopped
2 garlic cloves, smashed and chopped
1 tablespoon chopped parsley
1 1/2 pounds ground beef
Pinch of thyme
Salt
Pepper
1 1/2 cups chopped tomato
3 tablespoons tomato paste
4 cups hot mashed potatoes, divided (use left-over, freshly made from scratch, or instant from a box)
3 tablespoons melted butter

Heat oil in sauté pan. When hot, add onions, garlic, and parsley; mix and cook 3 minutes over medium heat. Add beef and thyme; mix well. Continue cooking 5 to 6 minutes over medium heat. Stir occasionally and season with salt and pepper to taste. Add tomatoes and tomato paste; cook 4 to 5 minutes over low heat. Spread half of mashed potatoes in bottom of large non-stick sprayed-baking dish. Cover with beef mixture. Spread remaining potatoes over top and pour on melted butter. Bake at 375° for 25 to 30 minutes, till all is warmed completely through and potato-topping has nice color.

A Conversation with the Cook... "Vinegar can remove spots caused by tomatoes. Soak the spot with vinegar and wash as usual."

✧

Angie's Hot Chicken Salad
Makes 6 servings

3 cups cooked, diced chicken
1 cup mayonnaise
1 teaspoon grated onion
2 cups thinly sliced celery
3 teaspoons lemon juice
1/2 cup slivered almonds
1 cup toasted bread crumbs or cubes
1/2 cup grated cheese

Mix all ingredients together except toasted bread crumbs and cheese. Put in greased casserole dish. On top put the cheese and toasted bread crumbs. Bake in 350° oven for 30 minutes.

A Conversation with the Cook... "Slip your hand inside a small sandwich bag and you have a perfect mitt for greasing your baking pans and casserole dishes."

Angie's Seafood Hot Dish

Makes 6 to 8 servings

For Casserole:
8 ounces bulk-style sausage
6 ounces crab meat, rinsed and drained
8 ounces shrimp, tenderly cooked
1 (10.75ounce) can cream of mushroom soup
4 ribs celery, sliced
1 green pepper, ribbed, seeded, and chopped
1 cup wild rice, cooked
1 (4 ounce) jar pimiento, chopped
1 (8 ounce) can sliced mushrooms, drained

Cook and crumble sausage. Stir soup until smooth and creamy and add to sausage. Combine rest of ingredients; mix well. Pour into a lightly greased 2-quart casserole. Bake covered for 45 minutes at 350°. Serve with sauce in recipe that follows.

For Sauce:
8 ounces tiny shrimp, tenderly cooked
1 (10.75 ounce) can cream of mushroom soup
1 (4 ounce) can sliced mushrooms, drained
1 1/2 tablespoons cooking Sherry

Heat together shrimp, cream of mushroom soup, mushrooms, and Sherry to form a sauce. Pass this in gravy bowl to serve atop casserole.

A Conversation with the Cook... "Sherry and sea food go together like peas in a pod."

Easy and Good Beef and Biscuits
Makes 6 servings

1 1/2 pounds ground beef
1 onion, chopped
1 (15 ounce) can diced tomatoes
2 to 3 carrots, chopped
1 celery stalk, chopped
1 teaspoon salt
1/2 teaspoon basil
1/4 teaspoon pepper
2 to 3 cans water (use the diced tomato can)
1 can of tube biscuits, baked at dinner time

Brown the ground beef and onion; drain off the fat. Add remaining ingredients; cook until vegetables are fully cooked. Add water as needed. Place in casserole dish and bake at 350° for 25 minutes. Serve right from the oven with freshly baked biscuits or dinner rolls. Add a salad and you have a meal.

A Conversation with the Cook... "Nothing compliments a meal like a warm-from-the-oven dinner roll. Take advantage of all those good tube-biscuits and packaged dinner rolls from your market. I always keep a tube or two handy to pop in the oven 'when I want to bake' at the last minute."

"Whose biscuits I eat: his song I sing."
~A Grandmother's Proverb

Pork Casserole
Makes 6 servings

2 pounds lean pork, diced
1 large green pepper, ribbed, seeded, and chopped
1 medium onion, chopped
1 cup pimento, chopped
1 (10.75 ounce) can chicken soup
1 (10.75 ounce) can mushroom soup
1/2 pound noodles, cooked
1 (8 ounce) can corn, drained
Bread crumbs, for topping

Boil noodles, drain. Mix all ingredients together (except corn and bread crumbs). In non-stick sprayed casserole dish, put in 1/2 noodle mixture, then corn, then remaining 1/2 noodle mixture. Put bread crumbs on top and bake at 350° for 1 hour.

A Conversation with the Cook... "Pork, the other white meat, is a nice change from eating beef and chicken."

Chapter Six
Seventeen Super "Sides"... Hot Dishes to Complete Any Meal

✧

"There is no love sincerer than the love of food."
~ *George Bernard Shaw*

RECIPE INDEX

Shirley's Baked Hash Brown Side Dish ... 191
Mother's Scalloped Potatoes ... 192
Double-Baked Potatoes Parmesan ... 193
MaryAnn's Versatile Southwest Bean Bake ... 194
Corn Pudding ... 196
Mom's Asparagus au Parmesan ... 197
Dorothy's Cabbage Casserole ... 199
Betty's Celery Bake Side-Dish ... 200
Artichoke Heart Casserole ... 201
Spinach Quiche Pie ... 202
Madame's Yams ... 203
June's Baked Carrot Mold ... 204
June's Noodle-Kugel Pudding ... 206
Baked Hot Fruit Compote ... 207

Koopmann's Favorite Baked Dish ... 209
Audra's Potato Broccoli Bake ... 210
Brown Sugar Tomato Bake ... 211

Shirley's Baked Hash Brown Side Dish

Makes 8 servings

2 pounds frozen hash browns, thawed
1/2 cup melted butter
Salt and pepper to taste
1 small or medium onion, chopped
1 (10.5 ounce) can cream of chicken soup, undiluted
1 pint sour cream
2 cups shredded Cheddar cheese
2 cups crushed corn flakes
1/4 cup additional melted butter

Combine first 7 ingredients in a bowl. Lightly grease a 9 x 13-inch pan and pour in hash brown mixture, spreading evenly. Mix together crushed corn flakes with 1/4 cup melted butter and sprinkle evenly over top of casserole. Bake at 350° for 45 minutes.

A Conversation with the Cook... "Shirley was a great cook and her hash brown casserole was requested for many a pot luck and buffet table!"

> *"Bear in mind that you should conduct yourself in life as at a feast."*
> *~Epictetu, philosopher*

Mother's Scalloped Potatoes
Makes 8 servings

4 large potatoes, peeled, thinly sliced, par-boiled for 5 minutes, and drained
Salt and pepper, to sprinkle over potatoes
1 package of Swiss cheese slices
1 medium onion, thinly sliced
Dijon-style mustard, to taste
1 cup dry white wine (or water)
1/2 cup dry bread crumbs
1/3 cup Parmesan cheese
Butter

Butter a shallow glass baking dish. Layer in a third of the potatoes; sprinkle with a little salt and pepper; then layer on half of the Swiss cheese slices. Lightly spread with mustard and sprinkle on half of the sliced onion. Repeat layers. Top with final third of potatoes. Pour over the wine or water. Mix the bread crumbs and Parmesan together and sprinkle over top. Dot with butter. Cover with foil and bake at 350° for 40 minutes; remove foil and bake, uncovered, for 15 minutes more to brown and crisp topping.

A Conversation with the Cook... "For a heartier variation, try this recipe with Cheddar cheese, or, for a creamier variation try Gruyere cheese...any way you do it, it comes to the table as a good old-fashioned family favorite."

Double-Baked Potatoes Parmesan
Use 1 potato per person, plus 1 extra to the batch

Nice sized baking potatoes, 1 per person (plus 1 additional, for extra pulp)
Milk
Butter
Salt and white pepper
Parmesan cheese
Additional butter
Additional Parmesan cheese

Wash potatoes and pierce with tines of a fork before putting in oven. Bake at 350° for 60 to 90 minutes, or until interiors, when pierced with a fork, are very tender. Remove from oven and cool slightly for ease of handling. Cut off upper thirds of potatoes (for chubby servings) or cut potatoes in half horizontally (for shallower servings). Remove pulp from skins, being careful not to rip skins that are going to be filled, and put pulp in a mixing bowl. Place reserved skins in an oven proof baking dish or on a cookie sheet and set aside. Mash pulp with the additions of milk, butter, Parmesan cheese to taste, salt and white pepper to taste—as if making stiff mashed potatoes. Generously mound the mashed-potato mixture back into the reserved potato skins. Sprinkle with additional Parmesan and dot with butter. ((For convenience you can make ahead to this point and store (wrapped) in the refrigerator, or even the freezer!)) Return stuffed potatoes to 350° oven and bake again until warmed through, and topping is golden brown.

A Conversation with the Cook... "Also known as 'twice baked potatoes' these are my daughter's favorite and make a special alternative to ordinary mashed potatoes ... easy to serve and easy to eat! A delightful variation of this dish is made by my friend, June, who uses generously sized red-skinned potatoes, omits the Parmesan cheese, and just dots the top of each stuffed potato with a little butter and a sprinkling of freshly snipped chives from her garden."

✧

MaryAnn's Versatile Southwest Bean Bake
Makes 6 to 8 servings

4 slices bacon
1 cup diced onion
1 teaspoon minced fresh garlic
1 (2 ounce) jar chopped pimiento, do not drain
1/8 teaspoon oregano
1 (15 ounce) can Bush's® black beans, drained and rinsed
1 (15 ounce) can Bush's® Great Northern beans, pink or pinto beans, drained and rinsed
1/2 cup mild picante sauce or chunky salsa
1 cup chicken broth
1/2 teaspoon salt
1/8 teaspoon pepper

In skillet fry bacon strips over medium heat until crisp. Remove bacon to paper towel. Drain. Cool then crumble. Pour off all but 1 teaspoon bacon fat from skillet. Add onion and garlic, stirring and cooking until onion is translucent, about 3 minutes. Remove skillet from heat, add pimientos, oregano, beans, picante sauce, chicken broth, salt, and pepper. Cook to heat through. Place mixture in non-stick sprayed 1 1/2 -quart casserole dish. Sprinkle crumbled bacon over top. Bake at 350° for 25 minutes or until dish is heated through.

A Conversation with the Cook... "For easy clean-up place some wax paper under the paper towel so bacon grease doesn't leak through to your counter. Note* omit the bacon and change the broth to vegetable broth and you have an alternative vegetarian side dish."

Corn Pudding
Makes 6 servings

3 cups canned corn, drained
2 tablespoons flour
1/4 teaspoon salt
1/2 teaspoon sugar
1/4 teaspoon paprika
1 teaspoon parsley, minced
2 farm fresh eggs, beaten
1 cup milk
4 tablespoons butter, melted

Mix all ingredients. Pour into buttered baking dish. Bake at 350° for 30 minutes, or until set.

A Conversation with the Cook... "You may determine the age of an egg by placing it in the bottom of a bowl of cold water. If it lies on its side, it is strictly fresh. If it stands at an angle, it is at least three days old; and ten days old if it stands on end. If you've lost track of the expiration date on the container, better to discard and buy fresh."

"My mother's menu consisted of two choices:
Take it or leave it."
~Buddy Hackett

Mom's Asparagus au Parmesan
Makes 6 servings

5 cups cold water
2 large bunches fresh asparagus, pared, washed, stalks snapped"
   of tough bottoms
1/2 cup grated Parmesan cheese
1 1/2 cups heated light white sauce (see recipe)
1/4 teaspoon nutmeg
1 lemon's squeezed juice
Salt
White Pepper
Paprika
1 recipe White Sauce

Pour water into roasting pan; add lemon juice and salt. Bring to boiling on stove top. Add asparagus to hot water and cook 8 to 10 minutes over medium heat, until just barely fork tender. When asparagus is cooked, remove and transfer to baking dish. Mix half of cheese and the nutmeg into white sauce. Pour white sauce over asparagus. Sprinkle top with remaining cheese and paprika. Bake 7 to 8 minutes in 375° oven, until all is warmed through and sauce is bubbly.

White Sauce
Makes 2 cups

2 cups milk
2 tablespoons butter
3 tablespoons flour
Salt and White pepper, to taste

Pour milk into saucepan and bring to boiling point. Remove and set aside. Heat butter in separate saucepan. When hot, add flour and mix well. Cook 2 minutes over low heat. Incorporate warmed milk into flour very slowly; stir constantly. Season sauce well with salt and white pepper. Continue cooking 10 minutes over low heat, never bringing to a boil, and stirring frequently. Your sauce is now ready for the asparagus recipe.

A Conversation with the Cook... "The first batches of fresh asparagus always heralded spring in our household and Mom couldn't wait to make her favorite way of cooking this seasonal delight. Whenever I make 'her dish' I think of Mom and all the wonderful cooking tips she passed on to me. Inherited recipes can be a wonderful way to preserve and remember our family traditions ... what 'heirloom recipes' do you have tucked away in your recipe box?"

Dorothy's Cabbage Casserole
Makes 8 side servings

1 large head of cabbage, cut up, par boiled, and drained
1 cup grated Cheddar cheese
1 (10.5) ounce can cream of mushroom soup

Mix all and pour into a buttered casserole dish. Bake at 350° for 45 minutes. Serve as a side dish with holiday meals.

A Conversation with the Cook... "Straight forward and uncomplicated (just like Dorothy) this makes a tasty European-style side-dish."

Betty's Celery Bake Side-Dish
Makes 8 side servings

1 bunch celery, stalks trimmed, de-veined, and cut into julienne (very thin strips, about 1/8 to 1/4-inch thick by 2 to 3-inches long, or as the French say, "the size of matchsticks")
1 Spanish onion, thinly sliced, julienne style
1/2 teaspoon each: cumin and ground coriander spice
1/2 cup pecan halves, toasted in a dry skillet over medium heat
Salt and white pepper to taste
2/3 cup vegetable or chicken broth
2/3 cup half-and-half cream
1/3 cup dry bread crumbs
1/4 cup grated Parmesan cheese
Butter

Toss sliced celery, onion, spices, and toasted pecans to mix, and pour into a buttered casserole dish. Season with a little salt and white pepper to taste. Mix broth and cream together and pour over celery mixture. Mix breadcrumbs and Parmesan together for a crumbly topping and sprinkle evenly over casserole. Dot with butter. Bake at 400° until celery is fork tender and topping is browned—about 40 minutes. Serve warm as a side dish with holiday meals.

A Conversation with the Cook... "Let celery find its way to your table in other than just the crudités and dip platter! Baked celery makes a perfect little side-dish for a holiday meal."

Artichoke Heart Casserole
Makes 4 to 6 servings

1 (9 ounce) package frozen artichoke hearts, cooked, cooled, and cut into bite size pieces
2 slices bread, whirled in blender to make soft crumbs
2 eggs, lightly beaten
1/2 teaspoon each: garlic salt, basil, oregano, marjoram
1/4 teaspoon white pepper
1/4 cup diced green onion, including tops
1/3 cup shredded Cheddar cheese
1/4 cup dry white wine
1/3 cup additional shredded Cheddar cheese, for topping

Toss all ingredients (except last Cheddar cheese) together lightly in a bowl and spoon into buttered, shallow casserole dish. Sprinkle on additional cheese as a topping. (Can make in advance to this point and refrigerate, covered.) Bake at 350° until warmed through, eggs are set, and cheese has melted—about 20 minutes. (If you have assembled the dish ahead and stored in refrigerator, and are going to go from cold directly to the oven, extend the cooking time.)

A Conversation with the Cook... "Always when you have assembled something ahead of time and stored in the fridge, count on extending your cooking time by about 10 to 15 minutes. Or pre-heat your oven 25° hotter than recipe calls for; put the chilled item in to cook, close oven door, and turn down setting to temperature called for in the recipe. That first little extra burst of heat will quicken the cooking process."

Spinach Quiche Pie

Makes 8 wedges

Filling:
1 pound spinach, cooked, drained, chopped
1/2 onion, chopped
1 clove garlic, mashed and mince
2 tablespoons butter
6 ounces mozzarella cheese, shredded
3 eggs, beaten
3/4 cup milk
1 teaspoon all purpose season-salt

Other stuff:
1 (9-inch) ready-made pie shell
1 to 2 fresh tomatoes, sliced thin (you will need 8 slices)
1/4 cup Parmesan cheese
Butter

Sauté cooked spinach, onion, and garlic in the 2 tablespoons butter until excess moisture has evaporated. Mix together mozzarella, eggs, milk, and seasoning-salt, and add to sautéed mixture, mixing well. Pour filling into pie shell. Decorate with 8 slices of fresh tomato, laid on top of filling around outer edge of pie. Sprinkle top of pie with Parmesan cheese and dot with butter. Bake at 425° for 15 minutes, then at 350° for 20 minutes more until firm. Let stand 10 minutes before serving, to make for easy cutting. Cut into 8 wedges, each wedge including a tomato slice. Serve as a hearty side dish or a light entrée with a fresh fruit platter and muffins.

A Conversation with the Cook... "This is my favorite quiche recipe, and I love the contrasting colors of the bright red tomato against the dark green filling. This is an example of color and presentation enhancing the dish."

✧

Madame's Yams
Makes 8 to 10 side-dish servings

4 large fresh yams, peeled, diced, cooked and drained
4 tablespoons butter
Pinch salt
Whipping cream
3/4 cup brown sugar
1 (medium size) can crushed pineapple, drained well
1 bag miniature marshmallows

Boil peeled and diced yams in a large pot until tender. Drain and transfer into large mixing bowl. Add butter, salt, and whipping cream and whip with mixer to desired consistency. Should be the same consistency as mashed potatoes. Transfer mashed yams to greased 9 x 13-inch glass baking dish and top with brown sugar. Drain the pineapple well and top over the casserole. Spread on the bag of mini marshmallows. Bake, uncovered, at 350° until marshmallows are golden brown, and casserole is heated through. Serve warm, being careful that the marshmallows are not too hot.

A Conversation with the Cook... "Be sure to use fresh yams, rather than canned for Madame's Casserole ... the end result is so much fluffier and tastier. For convenience the casserole can be assembled ahead of time, covered with plastic wrap, and stored in the fridge ... baking time will be longer when transferred straight from fridge to oven. I lovvvve this casserole and my friend Donna makes it the best!

For another fabulous side dish try June's Carrot Mold that follows! June's recipe makes a great addition to any fancy dinner—especially where kids and vegetables are concerned! "

⟡

June's Baked Carrot Mold

Makes 6+ serving slices, garnished with steamed peas

1 cup solid shortening (Crisco®)
1/2 cup brown sugar
1 1/2 cups finely grated raw carrots
3 eggs, separated
1 cup flour
1 teaspoon baking powder
1/2 teaspoon **each:** salt and baking soda
1 tablespoon fresh lemon juice
1 tablespoon water
Butter, for greasing mold
Cornflakes, crushed very fine, for "crumbing" mold
Cooked peas, at serving time, to put in the center of the mold

Cream together sugar and Crisco®. Add egg yolks and grated carrots, mixing well. Sift and add all dry ingredients, then lemon juice, then water, mixing well. Whip egg whites stiff and gently fold into carrot mixture. "Grease and crumb" a 4-cup ring-gelatin-mold. Do this by liberally buttering interior of mold and coating completely with very fine cornflake crumbs. Pat the crumbs onto the sides, coating mold completely. Carefully pour in the carrot mixture. Put the filled mold into a pan of water (this is called a "water bath"). The water should be about 1-inch deep. Bake (in the water bath) in 350° oven for 15 minutes, then raise temperature to 375° and continue baking 35 to 45 minutes more, or until mold is set. Remove mold from oven and loosen around edges of mold with a knife. Un-mold by inverting onto a serving plate. Fill the center of mold with steamed peas. Serve everything warm, as a fancy side vegetable. *Note:* recipe can be made ahead and freezes well, as do leftovers.

A Conversation with the Cook... "Who says a vegetable can't be fun to eat..."

June's Noodle Kugel Pudding
Makes 10 or so servings

16 ounces medium or wide noodles, cooked and drained
1 (16 ounce) carton cottage cheese, small curd
1 (16 ounce) carton sour cream
4 eggs, lightly beaten
2 cups milk, lightly warmed
1 tablespoon sugar
1 teaspoon salt
1 stick butter, halved, both halves melted
Additional sour cream, at serving time

Melt 1/2 stick butter and pour into a 9 x 13-inch baking dish to coat. Set aside. In a bowl mix cooked noodles, cottage cheese, sour cream, sugar, and salt. Set aside. Add eggs to warmed milk and mix well. Add egg/milk mixture to noodle mixture and mix. Mixture will be slightly "loose." Pour into the buttered baking dish, distributing evenly. Drizzle remaining melted butter over the top of the casserole. Bake at 350° for 1 hour and 15 minutes. Cut into squares and serve warm, topped with sour cream.

A Conversation with the Cook... "I have a darling neighbor who introduced me to this wonderful dish. Sometimes when I come home from work, I'm thrilled to find a treat of June's Noodle Pudding waiting at my door. One day when I was doing my shopping I noticed that my local deli had Noodle Kugel—in desperation I ordered a big slab (at great expense mind you). June had been on some hiatus from cooking her usual treats and I was in the middle of a sad case of kugel-withdrawal. With great anticipation I hurried home, to have my prized kugel—well, wasn't I disappointed! Nothing can match June Kurzon's Noodle Pudding! Moral of the story—when you've had the best, nothing else will do."

✧

Baked Hot Fruit Compote
Makes about 10 side-servings

1 medium size can pineapple slices
1 medium can peaches
1 jar apple rings
1 medium can pears
1 medium can apricot halves
1 stick butter
2 tablespoons flour
1/2 cup brown sugar, packed
1 cup Sherry

Drain all fruits and arrange in buttered casserole dish. In a double boiler*(see note) make a thick sauce with the butter, flour, brown sugar, and Sherry. Pour over the fruit. Cover with plastic wrap and refrigerate overnight. Heat oven to 350° and bake till hot and bubbly, about 30 to 40 minutes. Serve warm as a side dish with roasted chicken, duck, turkey, goose, and pork.

A Conversation with the Cook... "This Fruit Compote is the most awesome side dish I have found for holiday meals and as an accompaniment to poultry and wild fowl. If you want to wow your friends this is it! If you are not a Sherry lover, reserve 1 cup of fruit juices from the drained cans and use as a substitution for the Sherry."

*A Note about Double-boilers...*If you do not have a double boiler*—make one! Use a bowl, snuggly sitting over a sauce pan of steaming water. Or place a sauce pan in a shallow simmering water-bath in a larger pan. Either option works beautifully.

"Never trust a skinny cook."
~unknown

Koopmann's Favorite Baked Dish
Makes 6 to 8 servings

1 package frozen broccoli
1 package frozen cauliflower
1 package frozen Brussels sprouts
1 (8 ounce) jar Cheez Whiz®
1 (10.75 ounce) can cream of mushroom soup
1 (16 ounce) can Durkee® onion rings

Place vegetables in baking dish. Mix Cheez Whiz® and soup together and spread over top of vegetables. Bake for 2 hours at 350° with the dish covered. Top with Durkee® onion rings and bake 10 minutes more, uncovered.

A Conversation with the Cook... "I had to include this recipe in this section because it is a wonderful addition to any meal. My family requests this dish every Thanksgiving, but I also make it often throughout the year."

"A dish doesn't have to be fancy to be good."
~MaryAnn

Audra's Potato Broccoli Bake
Makes 6 to 8 servings

3 tablespoons butter, divided
2 tablespoons all-purpose flour
1 teaspoon salt and 1/4 teaspoon ground black pepper
1/2 cup each: onion and bell pepper, chopped fine and sautéed in 2 tablespoons butter until soft)
2 cups milk
1 (3 ounce) package cream cheese, cubed
1/2 cup shredded Cheddar cheese
16 ounces (about 4 cups) frozen hash brown potatoes, thawed
2 cups frozen chopped broccoli, cooked and drained
1/4 cup fine dry bread crumbs

In saucepan over medium-low heat, melt 2 tablespoons butter; blend in flour, salt, pepper, and milk. Cook and stir until bubbly. Add cream cheese and Cheddar, stirring until melted. Stir in potatoes. Spoon half of mixture into a shallow buttered baking dish, about 10 x 6 x 2-inch or 8 x 8-inch square. Top with broccoli, sautéed onion and bell pepper. Spoon remaining half of potato mixture over the broccoli layer. Cover and bake at 350° for 30 to 35 minutes. Melt final tablespoon of butter and mix with bread crumbs; sprinkle around edges of casserole. Bake, uncovered, 10 to 15 minutes longer.

A Conversation with the Cook... "A hearty side dish, this could be served equally as well as a vegetarian entrée." *~recipe courtesy of Audra LeNormand, Liberty Texas*

Brown Sugar-Tomato Bake
Makes 6 servings

5 to 6 cups rustic bread, crusts removed, cubed to 1–inch
1 stick butter, melted
1 (14.5 ounce) can whole tomatoes, with juice
1/3 cup water
1/4 cup Sherry
1 tablespoon tomato paste
2/3 cup packed brown sugar
Dash each: salt and pepper
Dash of Tabasco®
Dash of Worcestershire sauce

Toss bread cubes with melted butter; place in a greased 13 x 9-inch glass baking dish. In blender or food processor puree canned tomatoes with their juice. Pour into saucepan; add remaining ingredients and bring to simmer. Pour simmering mixture over bread cubes in baking dish. Bake uncovered, at 400° until pudding sets and edges begin to "caramelize"—about 35 to 40 minutes. Let rest 5 minutes before serving.

A Conversation with the Cook... "I love to use brown sugar in recipes. Its deep, rich, caramel-y flavor adds such depth to what could be an ordinary dish. Often when a recipe calls for sugar I will use a mixture of half brown and half white, just to enrich the flavor."

Chapter Seven
"Outside the Oven" ... Adding that Special Touch to Your Meal

✧

*"I never met a recipe I didn't like.
And some have become life-long friends."
~Wendy Louise*

RECIPE INDEX

Lucile's Homemade Apple Sauce ... 215
Smooth Avocado Sauce ... 216
Mayonnaise Frenchaise ... 216
Crème Fraiche ... 217
MaryAnn's Tartar Sauce ... 218
Thousand Island Dressing, Dip or Condiment ... 218
Change-of-Pace Salsa ... 220
New Mexican Salsa Cruda ... 221
Corn Salsa ... 222
Sunny Summery Gelatin Mold ... 223
Terrific Tomato Aspic ... 224
Fresh Fruit Tray with "Frosted" Grapes ... 225
Frozen Cranberry-Cream Mold ... 227
Cranberry Chutney ... 228

Liz's Lemon Curd ... 229

Rose Wine Jelly ... 231

Mother's Grilled Garden Tomatoes ... 234

Carla's Raspberry Vinaigrette Salad ... 235

Donna's Homemade Baileys Cream After-Dinner Drink ... 236

Café Delmonico Dessert Coffee ... 237

Sun Tea ... 238

Copper Carrot Pennies ... 239

Marilyn's Glazed Carrots with Red Grapes ... 240

MaryAnn's Bean Salad or Relish ... 241

Betty's 25 Tomato Catsup ... 242

Tomato and Cucumber Salad ... 244

German Potato Salad for a Crowd ... 245

Marshmallow Mint Salad ... 246

Surprise Gelatin Salad ... 247

Dieter's Delight ... 248

Steven's Country Salad ... 249

Orange Sherbet Gelatin Salad ... 250

Creamed Onions ... 251

Macaroni Salad ... 252

Asparagus Molded Salad ... 253

Creamy Cheddar Corn and Broccoli ... 254

Lucile's Homemade Apple Sauce
Flexible recipe, make as little or as much as you like

Peeled and chopped tart apples (Granny Smith are good)
A little water
Sugar, to taste
Dash of cinnamon, to taste

In saucepan simmer all till tender. With mixer, potato masher, or fork mash to consistency desired, or leave chunky. Taste test to your liking for sweetness and cinnamon. Serve warm.

A Conversation with the Cook... "My mother-in-law used to simmer up a batch of applesauce at a moments notice, when she was making a pork roast or pork chops Amounts of ingredients are totally flexible. This also makes a great topping for pancakes and adds a nice touch to breakfasts. At its best served warm, but can be served cold too. Would be great with duck, goose, and sauerkraut dishes as well."

"When you've learned to cook like your Mother-in-law—then you are a good cook. When you learn to cook like your Grandmother, you are an excellent cook. When you put the two together you are an awesome cook."
~Wendy Louise

Smooth Avocado Sauce
Makes 1 cup or so of sauce

1 avocado, pitted
1/2 cup water
Minced garlic, to taste
Salt and white pepper, to taste
1 tablespoon fresh lemon juice

Blend on high until smooth. Use immediately.

A Conversation with the Cook... "Use this velvety-smooth sauce as a garnish, instead of traditional guacamole. This sauce would make a pretty compliment to our Terrific Tomato Aspic recipe (see page 224)."

Mayonnaise Frenchaise
Makes 3/4 cup

1/2 cup mayonnaise
1/4 cup French dressing

Whisk until blended thoroughly. Store in refrigerator. Use as an accompanying sauce for sea food, instead of traditional tartar sauce. Also a great sauce on steamed asparagus, aspics, and salads. Use immediately.

A Conversation with the Cook... "These 2 ingredients make a special sauce as tasty as it is pretty."

Crème Fraiche
Makes 1 "batch"

1 cup heavy cream (whipping cream)
2 tablespoons buttermilk or yogurt

Combine both in glass container, and let sit undisturbed, on a kitchen counter at room temperature to "cure." Let set for at least 5 to 8 hours, or overnight to thicken. Use in place of sour cream. Can refrigerate up to 1 week, covered in a glass container.

A Conversation with the Cook... "In every one of my cookbooks (it must be my 'French roots') I include a recipe for crème fraiche. I cannot tell you how many times I've read a recipe that says serve with crème fraiche—and they never include how to make it! It is such a delightful replacement for sour cream ... and there is just something 'cool' about making your own. Parisians regard it as a staple in their daily diet, and it is much prized over store-bought sour cream."

> *"The qualities of an exceptional cook are akin to those of a successful tightrope walker:*
> *an abiding passion for the task,*
> *courage to go out on a limb,*
> *and an impeccable sense of balance."*
> *~ Bryan Miller*

MaryAnn's Tartar Sauce
Makes 1 cup

1 cup mayonnaise
1 tablespoon pickle relish
1 tablespoon capers, chopped (find capers in the condiment or specialty section of your market)
1 tablespoon minced onion
1/4 teaspoon sweet Hungarian paprika

Mix all and store in refrigerator. Serve with fish. Can store up to 3 days in refrigerator.

A Conversation with the Cook... "Serve this homemade tartar sauce with my Golden Fish Puffs (see page 54) or any other fish dish."

Thousand Island Dressing, Dip, or Condiment
Makes 1 1/2 cups

1 cup mayonnaise
1/4 cup chili sauce
2 tablespoons finely chopped pimento-stuffed green olives
2 tablespoons **each:** green, red, yellow bell peppers, minced
1/4 teaspoon Worcestershire
1/4 teaspoon cayenne
1/4 teaspoon sweet Hungarian paprika
1 tablespoon milk or cream, if desired

Mix all. Store in refrigerator. Keeps up to 1 week.

A Conversation with the Cook... "1000 island dressing makes a tasty variation from traditional tartar sauce, for serving with fish. Also try tossing your potato salad with it ... substitute the mayonnaise with Miracle-Whip® and you have an egg-less sauce ready-made for your salads and suitable for picnics and/or al fresco dining when food-temperature-safety is a consideration."

Change-of-Pace Salsa
Makes about 2 cups

1 cup finely chopped fresh peaches (or nectarines)
1 cup seeded and peeled, chopped cucumber
2 or 3 greens onions, chopped (including tops)
2 tablespoons snipped parsley
1 tablespoon sugar
1 tablespoon salad oil
1 tablespoon vinegar
1 tablespoon minced, fresh ginger root

Mix all and chill. Serve as a relish. Best if made fresh. Store in fridge.

A Conversation with the Cook... "Salsa can be so much more than chopped tomato and onion. Try this Caribbean style salsa with fish, shrimp, poultry, and even as a refreshing dip for chips."

A Special Note: **When storing acidic dishes**, relishes, condiments, salads, and such dishes as found in this chapter, it is best to store in non-metallic dishes. Lemon juice, lime juice, citrus juices, pineapple juice, vinegars, and especially tomatoes can interact with metallic containers. Once prepared and assembled, acidic mixtures and ones containing tomatoes should be stored in glass containers or plastic freezer containers. Just remember acid and metal don't mix. Tomatoes and metal don't mix.

New Mexican Salsa Cruda
Makes 2+ cups

3 tomatoes
4 green onions, including tops
1 small can black olive slices, drained
2 green chilies, seeded and chopped
Salt and freshly ground pepper to taste
2 tablespoons wine vinegar
1 tablespoon olive oil

Crudely chop all ingredients and mix. Serve with tortilla chips, or as a cool crisp salsa with entrees. Best if made fresh. Store in fridge.

A Conversation with the Cook... "This is a fantastic salsa that lends a fresh, lean, clean, crisp accent to any south-of-the-border dish. It also makes a great dip for an appetizer served with chips. And it makes a great garnish, next to a strata or baked cheese dish. Try this as an accent with the Corn Pudding on page 196."

Corn Salsa
Makes about 3 cups

1 medium red onion, finely chopped
1 tablespoon sugar
1 cup red wine vinegar, to be drained later
1 medium zucchini, scrubbed and diced
1 cup yellow corn (use canned, drained; or frozen, thawed; or better yet, leftover corn on the cob)
2 tablespoons olive oil
1 teaspoon salt
1 teaspoon pepper
Dash cayenne
Dash paprika

Combine onion, sugar, and vinegar in a glass bowl; let marinate 30 minutes in refrigerator. Drain off vinegar and set aside. Mix remaining ingredients and toss with onion mixture in glass bowl. Store in refrigerator. Use like a corn-relish condiment with appropriate casseroles. Best if used first day.

A Conversation with the Cook... "This is a great way to use up leftover corn on the cob! Just cut kernels off the cob and use instead of canned or frozen, proceeding as recipe is written. This also is a healthy dip to be used with tortilla chips as a party appetizer."

Sunny Summery Gelatin Mold
Makes 6 servings

1 (3 ounce) package lemon Jell-O®
1 cup hot water
1 (8 ounce) can crushed pineapple, with juice
1 carrot, peeled and shredded
Pinch salt
Juice of 1/2 lemon

Dissolve the gelatin in hot water. Fold in remaining ingredients. Chill till set.

A Conversation with the Cook... "Simple. Sunny. Fun. Top each serving with a dab of mayonnaise and a sprinkle of paprika for color, or better yet a maraschino cherry. Kids love this one."

"If we noticed little pleasures,
as we notice little pains,
If we quite forgot our losses,
and remembered all our gains,
If we looked for peoples' virtues,
and their faults refused to see,
What a comfortable, happy, cheerful place,
This world would be."
~unknown

Terrific Tomato Aspic

Fits a 4 cup mold, makes 6 to 8 servings

2 envelopes Knox® gelatin
1 teaspoon sugar
1 (6 ounce) can Snap E Tom Cocktail®
4 more (6 ounce) cans Snap E Tom Cocktail®
1 teaspoon A1 Sauce®
3 tablespoons lemon juice
1/2 teaspoon **each**: salt and onion juice
Sour cream, at time of serving
Sliced black olives, drained, at time of serving
Freshly snipped chives, at time of serving

Combine first 3 ingredients in small sauce pan and gently heat till gelatin dissolves. Remove from heat and stir in remaining ingredients—except for last 3, which are garnishes. Pour aspic into non-stick sprayed 4-cup mold. Refrigerate at least 2 hours, until mold is well set. Un-mold and garnish with sour cream, black olives, and chives. Serve cold. For a nice, colorful touch, replace the sour cream with a garnish of the Smooth Avocado Sauce (see page 216 for recipe) or Mayonnaise Frenchaise (see page 216 for recipe).

A Conversation with the Cook... "Zippy and snappy, this makes an out of the ordinary salad alternative. **To easily un-mold gelatins**, I like to invert the mold onto a serving plate, wrap with a hot towel, and jiggle until I hear the gelatin 'plop' out of the mold onto the plate. Immediately return to refrigerator until serving time."

Brook Noel's Fresh Fruit Tray with "Frosted" Grape Garnish

Ingredients for Fruit Tray:
Assorted melons: cantaloupe, honey dew, and watermelon, sliced
Tropical fruits: papaya, mango, and kiwi, sliced
Bananas
Strawberries, washed and dried
Blueberries, washed and dried
Seedless Grapes, both red and green
Lemon juice or Fruit Fresh® if needed

Slice and arrange an assortment of fresh fruits on your prettiest tray. Sprinkle with lemon juice or Fruit-Fresh® if needed. (You might need to do this if using apple slices or banana slices to prevent browning.) Hold off slicing and arranging your fruit until just before serving time, but make the Frosted Grapes a day ahead, or at least an hour ahead. If you feel harried in the kitchen, have a friend help you with this last minute slicing and assembling. (Kids love to help with the grape-frosting portion, which is done a day ahead of time.)

Ingredients for "Frosted" Grape Garnish:
1 egg white, slightly beaten
Granulated sugar
Selected fruit (in this case grapes) to "frost"
A clean pastry-basting brush

To make this decorative accent take a beautiful bunch of grapes and "frost" by brushing grapes (use a pastry or basting brush) with slightly beaten egg white (or beaten pasteurized-egg white). Then roll the brushed grapes in granulated sugar to coat. Set sugared grapes aside on waxed paper until dry. The grapes take at least an hour to dry. You can "frost" your grapes a day ahead of time and store in fridge until serving time, if you wish. The frosted grapes will make a beautiful accent for the center of your fruit tray. This technique can also be done with whole, dry strawberries and whole, dry blueberries, and is even beautiful on whole pears and apples, during the holiday season.

~Recipe excerpted from The Rush Hour Cook's Column, Mother's Day Menu, www.rushhourcook.com

Frozen Cranberry-Cream Mold
Makes 6 to 8 servings

1 standard can jellied cranberry sauce
2 tablespoons lemon juice
1 pint whipping cream
1/4 cup mayonnaise
1/4 cup powdered sugar

Mix together jellied cranberry sauce and lemon juice until blended and smooth. Pour into bottom of a non-stick sprayed mold. Put in freezer while you make the next layer. Whip the whipping cream, mayonnaise, and powdered sugar together until thickened as much as it will thicken, (This mixture will not whip up as stiff as whipped cream, but it will thicken and increase in volume some.) Pour this mixture into the mold and return all to the freezer, for several hours. To serve, un-mold onto a serving dish about 15 to 20 minutes before serving, so the mold thaws slightly.

A Conversation with the Cook... "This makes an absolutely dreamy, creamy dessert-style salad to serve with any meal. Great with spicy dishes, barbecued ribs, and any hot-saucy dish with which you want to refresh the palate. I always make it over the holiday season, and serve it in a pretty glass bowl, so I don't have to fiddle with un-molding it; and I'm always asked for the recipe."

Cranberry Chutney

Makes about 2 quarts, to be stored in small-sterilized Mason® or Kerr® jelly jars

2 pounds fresh cranberries
2 cups water
10 whole cloves
2 (2 1/2–inch sticks) cinnamon
1 (10 ounce) package dates, chopped into thirds
1/4 teaspoon salt
1 1/2 cup raisins
1/4 cup cider vinegar
1 1/2 cups sugar, or to taste
1 tablespoon Grand Marnier Liquor

Place cranberries and water in large pot and simmer until cranberries are tender and popped. Drain berries and return to pot. Add remaining ingredients. Cook, un-covered (over low heat) for 20 to 30 minutes to thicken. Carefully spoon while hot (mixture should be very thick) into sterilized jars (see page 231); wipe off any drips with a clean paper towel; and immediately screw on tops to vacuum seal. Unopened jars keep indefinitely in pantry. Use as a semi-sweet condiment-garnish with grilled meats and fowl. Once you've opened a jar, store in fridge.

A Conversation with the Cook... "Makes a tasty condiment with pork and roasted fowl ... and adds an extra 'meal-stretcher' serving-option to complete the meal. Also makes a wonderful hostess gift. Decorate the jar and add the recipe and contents on a cute little card. Your hostess will be very pleased."

Bonus Serving Suggestions: "This chutney makes a great appetizer served with a ripe, creamy Brie cheese and good crackers. Add a glass of good wine, and you'll think you're in France. For a European Dessert, serve the chutney, Brie, and crackers, along with Café Delmonico (see page 237) or just a good cup of after-dinner coffee or espresso. In Europe a cheese tray, along with its accompaniments, often ends the meal—proving that not all desserts have to be sweet."

◆

Liz's Lemon Curd
Makes 1 batch, approximately 2 cups

1 cup sugar
6 egg yolks
1/2 cup lemon juice
1 stick butter
1 to 1 1/2 tablespoons grated lemon peel

In medium saucepan, blend sugar and egg yolks. Add lemon juice gradually and blend. Cook mixture over low heat, stirring constantly until mixture coats back of spoon. (This process takes time so be patient.) Do not let mixture boil. Remove from heat. Skim off any foam if necessary. Cool slightly. Stir in butter and lemon peel to blend. Cool completely, stirring often to keep a film from forming on top. Your lemon curd is now ready to use. **For Tarts:** when cooled fill baked and cooled tartlet shells; chill and garnish tarts with kiwi slices. **For a Spread:** on scones, muffins, and breads, put lemon curd in sterilized jars (see page 231) and store in refrigerator, even though item is sterilized.

A Conversation with the Cook... "Although Liz likes to use her lemon curd as a filling for little tarts, I like to use it as a lemony spread on toast, scones, English muffins, biscuits, and breads. It also makes a nice little hostess gift for a weekend stay with friends. Use to spark-up breakfast breads with your morning coffee or as a snack-spread at tea time in the afternoon."

A Conversation about Gift Giving... "ALWAYS, when giving a food-gift from your kitchen, include a recipe card and the ingredients used—this will ease concern if the recipient has food allergies. Serving suggestions and storage directions should also be noted. You can even get fancy and build a 'theme basket' around your special treat—adding extras, such as pretty napkins, perhaps a serving dish or serving utensil, little plates, etc."

Rose Wine Jelly

Makes a small batch, to be stored in small-sterilized Mason® "jelly jars"

4 cups sugar
1 2/3 cups Rose wine
1/3 cup orange-flavored liqueur
2 tablespoons lemon juice
1 (6 ounce) bottle (or foil packet) of **liquid** fruit pectin

In a 4-quart heavy sauce pot, mix well the sugar, wine, orange liqueur, and lemon juice. Heat mixture to boiling over high heat on stove top, STIRRING CONSTANTLY. Immediately stir in pectin. Bring up to full "rolling boil" STIRRING CONSTANTLY, and cook 1 minute. Remove from heat and skim off any "foam." Immediately ladle into sterilized (see page 231) jelly jars; wipe off any drips on the rims with clean paper towel; and immediately screw on self-sealing tops. (I like to use Mason® brand jars and tops, found in my market or hardware store.) Let filled jars cool, undisturbed on kitchen counter—you will hear the tops "ping" as they cool and indent to make their seal. Store sealed jars in pantry; once opened store in fridge.

A Conversation with the Cook... "My mother-in-law, Lucile taught me to make jelly. Every summer we had the ritual of picking wild berries and making state-fair-quality, jewel-toned red raspberry and blackberry jellies. Jams would be strawberry, strawberry-rhubarb, and blueberry. I loved those afternoons—the ritual of sterilizing the jars, caps, and ladles. Hearing the lids "ping" as they sealed-in all that summer-goodness. Giggling and laughing at Lucile's side—comparing who made the clearest-jewel-toned jelly. (You can do it too—just get yourself a box of SureJell®, a lug of berries from the market, and follow the directions on the wonderful list of options in the package.)

I was so happy when I found this recipe for wine jelly, because that meant on a winter afternoon I could pursue my jelly making-again and give it as Holiday gifts. Delicately sweet, wine jelly is great on popovers or toast, yet great with lamb ... instead of that 'mint stuff' everybody is used to! Rhine wine also works well, but I like the delicate pink color of the Rose."

Sterilizing Jars and Utensils 101:

A Special Conversation with the Cook... "One of the most satisfying aspects of cooking is the 'putting-up' of jams, jellies, preserves, chutneys, relishes, and sauces, etc.—to be used at a later date, or to be given as gifts. To do this your containers (in this case glass jars) must be sparkling-squeaky-clean.

Start by putting your purchased jars, lids, and utensils through the dishwasher—or wash by hand in hot sudsy water, rinse thoroughly, and let air dry.

When you are ready to start cooking, place your largest-flat-bottomed pan on the stove top and fill with 1 -inch of water. Bring the water to boiling. Place all your jars (opening-side-down), lids (I like to use one-time, one-piece, self-sealing lids), and utensils, spoons, tongs, etc. in the boiling water; let them steam, bubble, and boil for at least 10 minutes. While they are sterilizing-away in the bubbling water, start cooking your recipe.

Lay out a clean towel or fresh paper toweling on a clean kitchen countertop. Pick a spot where your soon-to-be-filled-jars will be able to remain undisturbed as they cool with their final contents. With long handled tongs (that you sterilized in the bubbling water) carefully remove each jar and turn right side up on the towel-ed counter. Place all the lids there too. All steam and water droplets will evaporate out of the jars and off the lids, leaving them sterile and dry.

Proceed to fill your jars with your piping-hot recipe. Fill just up to the 'shoulder' of each jar—leaving about a 1/2-inch airspace between the 'neck' of the jar and the lid. (This airspace will create the vacuum seal.) You want to fill your jars while your recipe is very hot, so work quickly and carefully. Wipe off any spills or drips on the rims of the jars (with a clean paper towel)—as you need clean rims for a clean, safe seal.

After you've filled your jars, immediately screw on the sterilized self-seal lids. Let filled jars rest, undisturbed on the counter-top until they've cooled completely. As they cool, you will hear the lids 'ping' as they indent and form a vacuum seal. You can now safely store your treasures in the pantry, or give as gifts. Once you open a jar it must be stored in the fridge."

Mother's Grilled Garden Tomatoes

1 tomato-half per serving as a plate garnish, or 2 halves for a side vegetable

Tomatoes, cut in half
Grated Parmesan cheese
Dots of butter
Freshly snipped chives

Cut sun-ripened tomatoes in half, and squeeze out some juice and seeds. Place in foil-lined pan. Sprinkle on a liberal amount of grated Parmesan cheese and dot with butter. Garnish with chives. Turn oven onto broil-setting and place tomatoes several inches below broiler-element, grilling until hot and bubbly, but tomatoes still hold their shape. Use as a side vegetable and/or as a decorative garnish on each plated meal—especially good with steaks and chops.

A Conversation with the Cook... "Sometimes when I am alone, I make these as my main entrée—along with a crusty roll and a glass of wine, they make a great light dinner for a single person. Tomatoes are very healthy, full of vitamin A, C, folic acid and potassium—they make a great addition to any healthy diet."

> *"Food for thought is no substitute*
> *for the real thing."*
> *~Walt Kelly*

Carla's Raspberry Vinaigrette Salad
Makes 8 to 10 servings

8 cups torn Romaine
1 cup fresh raspberries
1/2 cup sliced almonds, toasted
1/2 cup seedless raspberry jam
Scant 1/4 cup cider or white vinegar
1/4 cup honey
2 tablespoons plus 2 teaspoons vegetable oil

Place torn romaine in salad bowl; top with raspberries and almonds. In blender, combine remaining ingredients and blend until smooth. Pour over salad just before serving and toss lightly. Serve on individual chilled salad plates with a couple extra berries as a garnish on top.

A Conversation with the Cook... "This salad was served to me on my 60th birthday, at a special dinner party ... I'm so sorry I had to wait 60 years to be introduced to this fabulous salad! It is the perfect complement to any meal."

A Conversation about Salads... "Greens may be washed and patted dry, and then placed in the salad-serving bowl. Dampen a couple paper towels and place over greens. Store in refrigerator until time of serving. The dressing can be made ahead and stored in a small covered jar; re-shake just before putting on salad. 'Dress' and toss the salad at the last minute, just before serving. A golden rule for salad dressing is "less is more." You want a light, glossy coating—not a puddle in the bottom of the bowl!"

✧

Donna's Homemade Baileys Cream After-Dinner Drink
Novelty recipe

Note* this recipe uses un-cooked eggs, must be refrigerated, and cannot be held beyond day of serving.

3 eggs
8 ounces Canadian whiskey (or brandy or rum)
10 ounces half-and-half cream
1 can Eagle brand® condensed milk
2 drops coconut extract
1 tablespoon Nestle Quick®

Put all ingredients in blender and mix well. Makes 1 quart. Refrigerate. Shake well before serving. Serve chilled, "on the rocks" (over ice), on the same day made.

A Conversation with the Cook... "Serve as an after dinner drink, in lieu of dessert. This one will knock your socks off."

Coffee Delmonico Dessert Coffee

Recipe written per serving

Directions:
1. Line each **heat-proof** mug with Kahlua liqueur and sugar.
2. Carefully flame 2 ounces of Brandy in a long-handled ladle, and gently pour into mug.
3. Swirl the flaming brandy around to ignite the mug and brown the Kahlua and sugar already in the mug.
4. When flames diminish fill mug with strong coffee.
5. Top with whipped cream, cinnamon, and shaved chocolate.
6. Make one at a time and serve immediately.

A Conversation with the Cook... "Use your best Maitre' D showmanship at tableside and serve as a flamboyant dessert-coffee."

> *"Enter with the entrée and bring down the curtain with dessert."*
> ~Wendy Louise

Sun Tea
Makes 1 gallon

A (1 gallon) clear glass, lidded jar (such as a large-pickle jar)
6 tea bags/ Fresh water/A sunny day

Fill jar to about 2 or 3 inches from top with fresh water and hang 4 to 6 tea bags over the rim. Put on lid and tighten, then screw back to slightly loosen, the lid will hold the hanging bags in place by their strings and tabs. Place jar, out on your patio, in direct sunlight and leave undisturbed for 3 to 4 hours. When tea has "brewed" to your liking remove bags, and store tea in the refrigerator. Serve chilled over ice.

A Conversation with the Cook... "If you have access to an herb garden, add a fresh sprig of rosemary, or several sprigs of mint directly to the jar to steep a very aromatic tea. Add a 2 to 3-inch slice of gingerroot to make a heady, spicy tea. You can also experiment with different types and combinations of herb and blended teas. Personally I just like to use Lipton® tea bags and pass wedges of lemon and my sugar bowl at serving time. I use tall glasses, plenty of ice, and my sterling iced-tea-spoons."

"A joy worth repeating
again and again
warm conversation, tea
and a friend."
~Miss Madeline

Copper Carrot Pennies

Makes 6 servings

Vegetables:
2 pounds carrots, sliced
1 green pepper, sliced
1 medium onion, sliced

Marinade:
1 (10.75 ounce) can tomato soup
1/2 cup olive oil
1 cup sugar
3/4 cup vinegar
1 teaspoon Worcestershire sauce
1/2 teaspoon salt
1/2 teaspoon pepper

Slice and cook carrots in salted water until just tender. Drain and cool. Combine marinade ingredients and pour over the mixed vegetables and cover. Refrigerate in glass bowl. Make ahead at least 8 hours.

A Conversation with the Cook... "Make this dish ahead of time because it gets better when it sets longer."

Marilyn's Glazed Carrots with Red Grapes

Makes 6 servings

2 pounds whole baby carrots
3 tablespoons butter
2 tablespoons sugar or brown sugar (packed)
1/2 pound sweet red seedless grapes, halved lengthwise
2 tablespoons chopped parsley

Simmer carrots in 1/2 cup water for 7 minutes; drain. In sauté pan melt butter; add sugar; add carrots; sauté for 4 minutes to glaze. Add halved grapes; sauté 2 minutes more. Sprinkle with fresh parsley and serve.
~recipe courtesy of Nancy, in honor of her sister Marilyn

A Conversation with the Cook... "This little side dish is a 'festival' of vegetable and fruit. Guaranteed to be a favorite with kids."

MaryAnn's Bean Salad or Relish
Makes 6 servings

1 (11 ounce) Bush's ® kidney beans
1 (11 ounce) Bush's® lima beans
1 (15 ounce) can cut green beans
1 (15 ounce) can cut yellow beans
1 onion, chopped fine
3 stalks celery, chopped fine
1 cup vinegar
1 cup sugar
1 cup water
1/2 teaspoon salt
1/2 teaspoon pepper

Bring the vinegar, sugar, water, salt, and pepper to a boil. Pour over the vegetables and mix. Refrigerate covered overnight, in non-metal container.

A Conversation with the Cook... "Three large stalks of celery chopped and added to about two cups of beans (navy, brown, pinto, lima, etc.) will make the beans easier to digest."

Betty's 25 Tomato 'Catsup'

Novelty recipe, makes about 2 pints to put up in jars

Step 1:
1 1/2 teaspoons whole cloves
1/4 teaspoon allspice
2-inch stick of cinnamon
1 teaspoon celery seed
1 bay leaf
1 cup white vinegar

In a small saucepan bring these 6 ingredients to a boil, cover, and remove from heat; set aside.

Step 2:
25 tomatoes, washed, cored, and quartered
1 onion, chopped
1/4 teaspoon cayenne

Into your largest pot, put the tomatoes, onion, and cayenne. Bring to boil and stirring often simmer for 15 minutes. Put this mixture through a sieve to get out all pulp, seeds, etc. ending with the purest tomato juice you can muster.

Step 3:
1 cup sugar

Add 1 cup sugar to the sieved juice and, again in your largest pot, simmer the mixture briskly for 2 hours, or until mixture is reduced by half.

Step 4:
4 teaspoons salt

Strain spices from step one's vinegar-mixture; add strained vinegar to simmering tomato mixture; add 4 teaspoons salt. Boil this final mixture for at least 30 minutes, stirring often. (Final "catsup" will be thinner than what you are used-to from bottled "ketchup.") Immediately transfer hot mixture into sterilized Mason® jars and let vacuum seal (see page 231). Store in refrigerator.

A Conversation with the Cook... "My mother, Betty, never 'put-up' preserves, or canned goods, or the like—but she did love to make homemade catsup. The first time, as I watched her scowling over the tomato spots accumulating on her fastidiously-washed, line-dried, sun-bleached (and ironed!) white blouse, as she tended the bubbling boiling mixture—I thought, *why?*...Well once I tasted my mother's "catsup" I knew why!"

Bonus Idea... "This would be a fun project to do with your kids, a 4-H group, or for a Girl Scout badge. Pick up the tomatoes from a farmer's market; go to the hardware store to get the Mason® jars; and be sure to wear old T-shirts when boiling up the batch! Everyone can take a turn at stirring and taste-testing and comparing 'homemade' with 'factory-made.'"

Tomato and Cucumber Salad

Makes 6 servings

5 medium tomatoes, sliced
1 cucumber, scored and thinly sliced
1 green onion, thinly sliced
3 tablespoons olive oil
3 tablespoons red wine vinegar
1/4 teaspoon salt
1/2 teaspoon black pepper
1/2 teaspoon crushed oregano
1/4 teaspoon crushed basil
1 tablespoon minced parsley

Place tomato slices, cucumber slices, and green onion in glass bowl. Mix together remaining ingredients; pour over salad. Chill about 1 hour before serving.

A Conversation with the Cook... "Fresh tomatoes keep longer if stored in the refrigerator with stems down. For cucumbers choose long, slender cucumbers for best quality. May be dark or medium green but yellowed ones are undesirable."

German Potato Salad for a Crowd
Makes 20 to 25 servings

8 pounds red potatoes, scrubbed but not peeled
1 pound bacon, diced
3 tablespoons flour
1/2 cup sugar
1 tablespoon salt
1/2 cup vinegar
1 medium onion, diced
2 1/4 cups water
Minced parsley (optional)

Cook potatoes in jackets (their peels) until tender; cool and peel. Dice bacon and fry over low heat until crisp. Drain, retaining fat; and dry bacon on paper toweling. Mix flour with 1/4 cup bacon fat, add sugar and salt, and stir well over low heat. Slowly add vinegar and 2 1/4 cups water. Cook, stirring until mixture starts to thicken; add onion. Slice the potatoes; combine with sauce and 1/2 of the crisp bacon. Sprinkle remainder of bacon on top. Minced parsley may also be added. Serve warm.

A Conversation with the Cook... "Potato salad is best made from potatoes cooked in their jackets. Small red waxy potatoes hold their shape when sliced or diced and do not absorb an excessive amount of dressing or become mushy."

Marshmallow Mint Salad

Makes 20 servings

1 (3 ounce) package lime gelatin
1 cup boiling water
1 (10.5 ounce) bag miniature marshmallows
1 (21 ounce) can crushed pineapple, with juice
1 (8 ounce) box butter mints
6 cups Cool Whip®

Dissolve gelatin in 1 cup boiling water; add marshmallows. Stir well until gelatin and marshmallows dissolve. Add pineapple and juice. Refrigerate for two hours, stirring often while mixture starts to congeal. Add Cool Whip®. Crush the mints with a rolling pin; fold mints into gelatin mixture. Pour into 13 x 9-inch freezer-safe dish and freeze overnight.

A Conversation with the Cook... "This is a crowd pleaser in every way. Try using different flavors of gelatin."

*"No mean woman can cook well.
Cooking calls for a generous spirit, a light hand,
and a large heart."
~ Paul Gauguin, painter*

Surprise Gelatin Salad
Makes 6 to 8 servings

1 (3.25 ounce) package regular vanilla pudding
1 (3 ounce) package lemon gelatin
1/2 teaspoon lemon juice
2 cups boiling water
1 (3 ounce) package raspberry gelatin
1 cup boiling water
1 (16 ounce) can whole cranberry sauce
4 ounces Cool Whip®

In saucepan, combine pudding mix, lemon gelatin, and 2 cups boiling water. Heat and stir until mixture boils. Stir in lemon juice. Set aside and chill until partially set. Meanwhile dissolve raspberry gelatin in 1 cup boiling water. Stir until gelatin is completely dissolved. Beat in whole cranberry sauce till dissolved; set aside. Add Cool Whip® to chilling pudding mixture by folding in gently; set aside again. Pour half of cranberry/raspberry mixture into mold. Spoon pudding/Cool Whip® mixture over. Top with remaining cranberry/raspberry mixture. Refrigerate overnight to fully set.

A Conversation with the Cook... "You can use a glass bowl if you don't have a gelatin mold. This is such a convenient dish because you can make it well ahead of time. Great for the holidays."

Dieter's Delight

Makes many servings, recipe may be halved

1 head cauliflower
1 bunch broccoli
2 (20 ounce) packages frozen peas, blanched
1 bunch celery
2 pounds carrot
2 cups sour cream
2 cups Miracle Whip® (also known as salad dressing)
1 package Knorr® vegetable soup mix

Cut vegetables into bite size pieces. Add peas and mix in salad dressing, sour cream, and soup mix. Stir all to mix and chill.

A Conversation with the Cook... "This makes a great salad for a large gathering or buffet table. For everyday consumption, you'll want to cut the recipe in half."

"My wife dresses to kill.
She cooks the same way."
~Henny Youngman, comedian

Steven's Country Salad
Makes 6 to 8 servings

Salad:
1 bunch fresh broccoli, washed, drained, broken into flowerets
1/2 cup chopped red onion
1 cup chopped celery
1 pound bacon, fried crisp, drained and crumbled
1/2 cup cashew nuts

Dressing:
3/4 cup mayonnaise
1/4 cup sugar
2 tablespoons vinegar

Combine salad ingredients together in a large mixing bowl; set aside. Combine dressing ingredients and toss with salad. Store covered in refrigerator in glass dish, to blend flavors. Can conveniently make ahead.

A Conversation with the Cook... "This is my son-in-law's favorite recipe that I make. Tastes great the next day."

Orange Sherbet Gelatin Salad
Makes 8 servings

2 (3 ounce) packages orange gelatin
1 cup boiling water
1 pint orange sherbet
1 (11 ounce) can mandarin oranges, drained
1 cup heavy cream, whipped

Dissolve gelatin in hot water; add sherbet and mix well. When partially set, add oranges and fold in whipped cream. Pour into a 1 1/2 quart ring mold or glass dish; chill until set.

A Conversation with the Cook... "Be sure the mandarin oranges are drained well otherwise they will make the salad soupy and it won't set correctly."

Creamed Onions
Makes 12 servings

1 cup sugar
1/2 cup white vinegar
1/2 cup water
2 1/2 tablespoons cornstarch
1 tablespoon butter
2 pounds sliced sweet onions
1 cup sour cream
Salt and pepper to taste

Mix sugar, vinegar, water, cornstarch, and butter. Bring to a boil stirring until mixture thickens. Let cool. Whip in sour cream then pour over sliced onions in a glass bowl. Toss and serve.

A Conversation with the Cook... "When peeling an onion, cut the bottom off first so the juices will go down and not bother the eyes; or refrigerate them before chopping. Also lemon juice will remove onion scent from hands."

"Mine eyes smell onions: I shall weep anon."
~All's Well That Ends Well, William Shakespeare

Macaroni Salad

Makes 12 servings

8 ounces macaroni
1 1/2 cups Cheddar cheese, shredded
1/2 cup pickle relish
3 hard-boiled eggs, chopped
1 tablespoon pimento, chopped
1/2 teaspoon salt
1/2 teaspoon pepper
3/4 cup mayonnaise
1 cup celery, finely chopped
1/3 cup green pepper, ribbed, seeded, and chopped
2 teaspoons onion, finely chopped

Cook macaroni according to package directions. Rinse in cold water. Drain well after rinsing. Add remaining ingredients to macaroni. Mix lightly. Cover and chill.

A Conversation with the Cook... "Add a teaspoon of oil to water when cooking macaroni and the macaroni won't stick together or stick to the pot. This salad is everybody's favorite."

Asparagus Molded Salad
Makes 6 to 8 servings

1 (10.75 ounce) can asparagus soup, undiluted
1 (3 ounce) package lime gelatin
1/2 cup cold water
4 ounces cream cheese, softened
1/2 cup mayonnaise
1/2 cup chopped celery
1 tablespoon grated onion
1/2 cup chopped green pepper
1/2 cup chopped pecans

Heat soup to boiling. Remove from heat and add gelatin. Stir until dissolved. Add cream cheese and mix until well blended. Add water and mayonnaise, beat until blended. Stir in remaining ingredients and turn into mold. Chill until set. Garnish with Mayonnaise Frenchaise (see page 216).

A Conversation with the Cook... "Use a fancy, decorative mold and let people guess what the secret ingredients are in this elegant salad. This very different salad mold would be most elegant with the Stuffed Crown Roast of Pork dinner (see page 147). You would certainly have a meal fit for a king."

Cheddar Corn and Broccoli
Makes 6 servings

1 cup chopped onion
1 tablespoon butter
1 cup cooked broccoli pieces
1 (15 ounce) can whole kernel corn, drained
1 (10.75 ounce) can condensed Cheddar cheese soup

In large saucepan, cook onion in butter until tender. Stir in remaining ingredients. Cook 10 minutes or until heated through, stirring occasionally.

A Conversation with the Cook... "This is one of my family's favorite side vegetables and makes an easy side dish to any meal—a no-fail dish for the beginner cook."

Chapter Eight
"Our Daily Bread"

✧

*"If you have but two pence left
take one to buy a loaf of bread
and the other to buy a hyacinth."*
~*old English proverb*

RECIPE INDEX

Sara's No-Fail French Bread ... 257
Mushroom Stuffed Crescent Rolls ... 259
Lemon Bread ... 260
Date Nut Bread ... 261
Bobbie's All Season Bread ... 262
Rhubarb Nut Bread ... 264
Corn Bread ... 266
Aunt Emma's Hot Corn Bread ... 267
I Slaved All Day Cheddar and Herb Biscuits ... 268
Caleb's Beer Bread ... 269
Cinnamon Muffins ... 270
Auntie Joan's Popovers ... 271
Liz's Soft-Baked Bread Sticks ... 272
Angie's Pumpkin Bread ... 274
Chocolate Banana Bread ... 275
Cinnamon Zucchini Bread ... 276

Butterhorns ... 277
Peach Coffee Cake ... 278
Banana Chocolate-Chip Muffins ... 280
Dottie's Blueberry Muffins ... 281
Dorothy's Strawberry Muffins ... 284
Sweet Potato Biscuits 285
Carrot and Pineapple Muffins ... 286
Sour Cream Coffeecake ... 287
Fresh Pretzels ... 288
Old Fashioned Corn Biscuits ... 290
Big Apple Pancake ... 291
Irish Oatmeal Bread ... 292
Cereal Coffee Cake ... 293

Sara's No-Fail French Bread
2 loaves

2 cups warm water (about 105°)
1 packet dry yeast, dissolved in 1/4 cup warm water
1 1/2 teaspoons salt
1 1/2 tablespoons sugar
6 cups sifted all-purpose flour

Put all but the flour in a large bowl. Stir. Beat in half of the flour. Beat in 2 cups more, 1 cup at a time, beating well each addition. Put half of the last cup of flour on work surface. Knead dough with hands, continually brushing on flour to work in. Keep kneading in the remaining flour until dough is smooth and not sticky, about 10 minutes. (To "knead" the dough, do so by folding half the dough toward you over the bottom half with floured hands, push dough away from you with the heels of your hands. Repeat and repeat, using more flour as needed. Dough should have a nice elastic, smooth feel to it.)

Put dough in a greased bowl, grease top lightly, and cover with a slightly damp towel. Set in a warm (about 80°) draft free place (oven works good) for about 1 1/2 hours—or until dough doubles in size. Punch dough down hard with hands and divide into 2 parts. Shape into 2 long loaves. Put shaped loaves into 2 French Bread Pans, or on a cookie sheet. Let rise again in warm place until doubled, about 45 minutes.

Score top of each loaf with diagonal slashes and bake in pre-heated 400° oven for 45 minutes, until good and crusty. Bake on middle rack, with a shallow pan of water on lower rack to humidify oven.

A Conversation with the Cook... "This can be a great Saturday afternoon project with the kids. Homemade bread is so gratifying, and although I'm not a good bread-baker I can make this one."

Mushroom Stuffed Crescent Rolls

Flexible recipe, estimate 2 rolls per person

1 tube of Pillsbury® style crescent rolls
6 or 7 fresh mushrooms, chopped fine (or use a small can of
   mushroom pieces from your pantry, drained and chopped fine)
1 green onion, including top, minced
1 tablespoon fresh parsley, minced
1 teaspoon snipped fresh chives, minced
1 tablespoon butter

Quickly sauté mushrooms, onion and herbs in butter to blend flavors and cook a little. Unroll crescent dough and separate along perforations. Distribute sautéed filling equally in the middle of each roll. Roll up each dough-piece to contain its filling. Bake as per package instructions, but just for 1 or 2 minutes longer (because of the filling). Serve in a tea-towel-lined basket to keep warm.

A Conversation with the Cook... "These little dinner rolls will melt in your mouth. Their 'surprise' filling just adds that extra touch! And speaking of extra touches, you might want to invest in a warming-stone bread basket (found at gourmet stores.) The stone is heated in the oven and placed in the bottom of the linen-lined basket to keep your breads warm all through dinner."

"Nature alone is antique and its oldest art the mushroom."
~*Thomas Carlyle*

Lemon Bread

Makes 1 loaf, baked in a 2-quart dish

Bread:
3/4 cup margarine
1 1/2 cups sugar
3 eggs
2 1/4 cup flour
1/4 teaspoon salt
1/4 teaspoon baking soda
3/4 cup buttermilk
Grated rind from 1 lemon
3/4 cup chopped nuts

Glaze:
The juice from the 1 lemon
1/2 cup sugar

Cream together margarine and sugar. Beat in eggs. Sift flour, salt, and baking soda together and add to batter alternately with buttermilk, mixing well each addition. Stir in rind and nuts. Pour batter into a greased and floured 2-quart baking dish. Bake at 325° for 1 hour and 20 minutes. Cool bread 15 minutes in dish, remove to serving plate, pierce top and spoon on glaze: To make glaze combine the lemon juice and sugar until smooth and drizzle over bread and into pierced holes.

A Conversation with the Cook... "This is such a versatile bread—good at breakfast, lunch, or dinner, or snack! Its sweet but tart flavor goes with almost any meal, but could be served as a dessert too."

✧

Date Nut Bread
Makes 2 loaves, better made a day ahead

1 (1/2 pound) package chopped dates
2 teaspoons baking soda
2 cups boiling water
1 stick butter
2 cups sugar
2 eggs
4 cups flour
2 teaspoons salt
1 cup chopped nuts

Combine dates, baking soda, and boiling water. Set aside to cool. Cream together butter and sugar; add in eggs 1 at a time. Mix flour and salt together. Add flour mixture and date mixture, alternately to the creamed mixture, blending each addition. Lastly fold in nuts. Divide into 2 greased loaf pans. Bake at 325° for 1 hour to 1 hour and 10 minutes. Cool loaves; remove from pans; wrap in foil. Refrigerate for 1 day before slicing.

A Conversation with the Cook... "This is one of my favorite holiday breads for serving and gift giving. Serve as thick slices with cold butter or cream cheese."

Bobbie's All Season Bread
Makes 2 loaves

3 cups all-purpose flour
2 teaspoons soda
1 teaspoon salt
1/2 teaspoon baking powder
1 1/2 teaspoons cinnamon
3/4 cup finely chopped nuts
3 eggs
2 cups sugar
3/4 cup vegetable oil
2 teaspoons vanilla
1 (8 ounce) can crushed pineapple, drained (and reserved)
2 cups prepared fruit or vegetable from the following list:
    for Apple Bread......2 cups peeled, cored, and shredded apple
    for Carrot Bread......2 medium carrots, peeled and shredded
        1 tablespoon of the drained pineapple juice
    for Zucchini Bread...2 cups, peeled, shredded tender zucchini

Combine first 6 ingredients; set aside. Beat eggs lightly in large mixing bowl. Add sugar, oil, and vanilla; beat until creamy. Stir in crushed pineapple and prepared fruit of choice (from list). Add-in dry ingredients, stirring only until moistened. Do not overwork batter. Spoon into 2 well-greased and floured 9 x 5 - inch loaf pans. Bake at 350° for 1 hour, or until wooden pick inserted in center comes out clean.
~recipe courtesy of Judy Brown, Midland Michigan

A Conversation with the Cook... "A favorite in the Brown family, any time of the year. Bake one loaf to enjoy now; freeze the other for later."

A Conversation about Butter... and a Bonus Recipe ... "There is just something special about the combination of bread and unsalted butter. Unsalted butter may also be purchased in whipped form, which is delightful. For another taste treat, with your mixer, whip together 1 stick of slightly softened unsalted butter, 1 to 2 tablespoons honey, and 1/4 teaspoon vanilla extract. Whip well, until blended and smooth. Store in refrigerator. Use your bonus-recipe **Honey Butter** on warm biscuits, breads, and muffins."

Rhubarb Nut Bread
Makes 2 loaves

1 1/2 cups light brown sugar
2/3 cup vegetable oil
1 egg
1 cup sour milk* (see note below)
1 teaspoon **each**: baking soda, salt, vanilla
2 1/2 cups flour
1 tablespoon baking soda
1 1/2 cups diced rhubarb
1/2 cup chopped pecans

In first (and largest) bowl mix together sugar, oil, and egg. In second bowl mix soured milk, baking soda, salt, and vanilla. In third bowl sift together flour and baking powder. Add mixtures from second and third bowls to first bowl, alternately, mixing well each addition to make the batter. Lastly fold in the rhubarb and nuts. Divide between 2 greased loaf pans (I like to use greased Teflon® pans). Bake at 325° for 1 hour. Cool before removing from pans.

A Conversation with the Cook... "**To sour the milk*** add 1 tablespoon of lemon juice or vinegar to 1 cup whole milk. The lactic acid will naturally 'sour' and thicken the milk. Soured milk can be used as a substitute when buttermilk is called for, or vice versa. So the next time your recipe calls for sour milk (or buttermilk) don't panic, because now you know what to do.

(You can also sour cream the same way, ending up with a homemade sour cream much like crème fraiche.)

Interestingly, on the same note but for a totally different purpose, a tablespoon of vinegar or lemon juice added to heavy cream or half-and-half makes a great base for coleslaw dressing.)"

Corn Bread
Makes 9 squares

1 cup yellow corn meal
1 cup flour
1/4 cup sugar
4 teaspoons baking powder
1/2 teaspoon salt
1 cup milk
1 to 2 eggs (depending on their size)
1/4 cup vegetable oil

Mix dry ingredients together. Mix wet ingredients together. Mix the two mixtures together. Bake in a greased 8 x 8-inch square pan, at 425° for 20 to 25 minutes, or until toothpick pierced in center comes out clean. Cut into squares and serve warm from pan.

A Conversation with the Cook...Bonus Recipe: "For a fun novelty muffin, bake one half of the corn bread recipe in greased mini-muffin tins. (In this case bake only for 12 to 15 minutes.) When the little muffins have cooled, split off the tops and hollow out a small well in the center of each muffin. (The small end of a melon-baller works well for this.) Put in a teaspoon of jellied cranberry sauce, and put the top back on each muffin. These **Mini Muffins with a Surprise** make a special treat—especially for children."

Aunt Emma's Hot Corn Bread
Makes 8 or so servings

1 cup corn meal
1/2 cup flour
1/2 teaspoon soda
1/2 teaspoon salt
1 small can cream style corn
1 cup grated Cheddar cheese
1/3 cup vegetable oil
2 eggs
1/3 cup grated onion
2 pod-hot, jalapeno peppers, seeded and diced fine
(*Note*ALWAYS when working with hot peppers, wash your hands well immediately after, being careful not to rub your eyes or mouth before doing so.)

Put first 4 ingredients in bowl and mix. Mix in the remaining ingredients, adding as listed. Spread into a well-greased heavy cast iron skillet. Bake for 30 minutes at 375°. Cut into wedges and serve.

A Conversation with the Cook... "My Aunt Emma says to use a big skillet so the batter isn't baked too thick. For really hot corn bread leave in a few of the jalapeno seeds to give it extra heat!" *~recipe courtesy of Judy Brown, Midland Michigan*

I Slaved All Day Cheddar and Herb Biscuits

Makes 8 servings

1 tube refrigerated biscuits
3 tablespoons butter or margarine, melted
1 tablespoon garlic powder, pepper, and dill (or any other mixed seasoning)
1 cup shredded Cheddar cheese

Melt butter and mix with seasonings. Brush butter over biscuits. Top biscuits with Cheddar cheese. Bake for 12 minutes in 375° oven, or as directed on package. Serve warm from the oven.

A Conversation with the Cook... "You can serve these biscuits without butter because they just melt in your mouth." ~*Brook Noel, The Rush Hour Cook*

> *"Life is hard. Make cooking easy"*
> *~The Rush Hour Cook, Brook Noel*

Caleb's Beer Bread
Makes 1 loaf

3 cups self-rising flour
3 tablespoons sugar
1 can beer

Mix thoroughly. Spread in greased loaf pan. Bake 1 hour at 350°. Bread is done when you knock on it and it sounds "hollow." Cool slightly before removing from pan.

A Conversation with the Cook... "This is purely a novelty bread and my son used to love it with a big bowl of chili. You must use self-rising flour for the recipe to work."

"Man does not live by bread alone."
~Moses

Cinnamon Muffins

Makes 1 dozen

2 cups flour
3 teaspoons baking powder
3 teaspoons cinnamon
1/4 teaspoon salt
2 eggs
1 cup milk
1/2 cup vegetable oil
1 cup brown sugar, packed
1 cup finely chopped nuts
1/2 cup raisins (optional)

In first bowl mix together first 4 ingredients. In second bowl mix together eggs, milk, and oil. Stir second mixture into first mixture. Then stir in brown sugar, then nuts, then raisins to form your batter. Bake in greased muffin tins at 375° for 15 to 17 minutes.

A Conversation with the Cook... "Instead of greasing my muffin tins, I like to use paper muffin-cup liners—you'll find these in the baking section of your market. They come in a standard size and a mini size. Also remember, even when using paper cups, to grease the **top** of your muffin tin—so those big puffy muffins don't stick when they bulge over. A good rule of thumb is not to fill your muffin cups more than 3/4 full—unless you are going for the coffee-café-look of giant muffins."

Auntie Joan's Popovers

Makes 1 dozen, standard-size muffin-tin popovers

1 cup flour
1/4 teaspoon salt
1 tablespoon sugar
1 tablespoon oil
1 cup milk
2 large eggs

Mix first 3 ingredients together. Mix second 3 ingredients together. Mix wet into dry until very smooth. Fill greased cups 1/2 full. (In this case do not use paper liners.) Bake on center rack at 400° for 30 to 40 minutes, depending on size of your muffin cups. DO NOT open the oven door while the popovers are baking, or you will have "poofed-plop-overs." As soon as you remove the popovers from the oven prick each one with a toothpick, to help prevent them from falling. Cool slightly before removing from pans.

A Conversation with the Cook... "There's just no question about it...good popovers are one of the finer things in life. Served with a homemade jam or jelly they are just divine. If you make them with any frequency, I would suggest investing in a good popover tin, which you can get at any fine gourmet outfitter."

Liz's Soft-Baked Bread Sticks
Makes 32 bread sticks, or 2 loaves of bread

6 to 6 1/2 cups unbleached flour
2 packages yeast
2 tablespoons sugar
1 tablespoon salt
1/4 cup vegetable oil
2 1/4 cups warm water
Coarse salt, at baking time

Mix together 2 cups flour, yeast, sugar, salt, oil, and water. Beat 2 minutes at medium speed. Add 1 cup flour; mix 1 minute longer. Add 3 cups flour, stirring with a wooden spoon. Knead dough on a floured surface for 5 to 10 minutes, using more flour as necessary. Rest dough in greased bowl, covered with a tea towel for 20 minutes. Punch down dough before shaping.

To shape, cut dough in half and then in half again. You should have 4 approximately 3 x 8-inch pieces of dough. Cut each into 8 pieces. Roll between hands to form bread stick shapes. Place on cookie sheets. Oil tops and cover with plastic wrap. Refrigerate for 2 to 24 hours to rise again before baking. (This is called the cool-rise method.) Remove from fridge and sprinkle rolls with coarse salt just before baking. Bake at 425° for 15 to 20 minutes.

A Conversation with the Cook... "Liz introduced me to these bread sticks on a picnic many years ago and I had to have the recipe. Liz also suggests that this recipe can be baked as 2 loaves of bread. To do so, shape dough into 2 loaves and place in greased loaf pans, oil tops, and cool-rise for the 2 to 24 hours, covered with plastic wrap just like the bread sticks. Adjust baking temperature to 400° and bake for 30 to 40 minutes."

Angie's Pumpkin Bread
Makes 2 Loaves

3 cups flour
1 1/2 cups sugar
2 teaspoons cinnamon
1 teaspoon baking soda
1/2 teaspoon salt
1 teaspoon nutmeg
3/4 teaspoon cloves
1/2 teaspoon baking powder
3 eggs
1 (16 ounce) can pumpkin
1 cup olive oil
1/2 cup chopped nuts

In a large bowl, mix flour, sugar, cinnamon, baking soda, salt, nutmeg, cloves, and baking powder. Mix in eggs, pumpkin, and oil until moistened. Stir in nuts. Pour into 2 greased loaf pans. Bake at 350° for 1 hour or until wooden pick inserted in the center comes out clean. Cool 5 minutes. Loosen sides of loaf pan; remove from pan. Cool completely before slicing.

A Conversation with the Cook... "All the flavor of a pumpkin pie packed into a loaf of bread. Moist, spicy, great with pork dinners in the fall."

"Bread is the warmest, kindest of all words.
Write it always with a
capital letter, as if it were your own name."
~author unknown

Chocolate Banana Bread

Makes 2 loaves

1 1/2 cups sugar
6 tablespoons butter
3 eggs
6 ripe bananas
1/2 cup milk
2 1/2 cups flour
1 1/2 teaspoons baking soda
1/4 teaspoon salt
1/2 teaspoon baking powder
1 1/2 cup baking cocoa

In a large mixing bowl, mash the bananas. Add all ingredients; beat on medium speed with electric mixer until well combined. Spray 2 loaf pans with non-stick cooking spray. Divide batter evenly. Bake at 350° for 50 minutes. Let cool for at least 5 to 10 minutes before removing from loaf pans.

A Conversation with the Cook... "You know how sometimes those bananas just begin to ripen too fast for you?—well they are perfect for baking!"

Cinnamon Zucchini Bread

Makes 2 loaves

3 eggs
1 1/2 cups sugar
1 cup vegetable oil
2 cups grated zucchini
2 teaspoons vanilla
3 cups flour
1/2 teaspoon salt
1 teaspoon baking soda
3 tablespoons cinnamon
1/2 teaspoon baking powder
1/2 cup chopped nuts

Beat eggs; add sugar and oil. Add zucchini and vanilla; mix well. Add remaining ingredients. Spray pans with Pam®. Divide into 2 large loaf pans. Bake at 350° for 50 to 60 minutes. Cool before removing from pans.

A Conversation with the Cook... "I often make this recipe and give the loaves as gifts."

Butterhorns
Makes 12

Rolls:
1 ounce cake yeast
1/4 cup warm water
3/4 cup + 2 tablespoons sugar, divided
1 cup butter, softened
2 cups flour
1/4 teaspoon salt
2 eggs, separated
2 teaspoons butter vanilla
1/4 cup chopped nuts
1 1/2 teaspoons cinnamon

Icing:
1 cup powdered sugar
1 teaspoon hot water
1/4 teaspoon each: vanilla and almond extract

Dissolve yeast in 1/4 cup warm water and 2 tablespoons sugar. Add flour, softened butter, and a little salt; mix as for pie dough. Add egg yolks, butter vanilla, and 1/4 cup sugar to the yeast mixture; mix well and divide dough into thirds. Roll out each third into a rectangle-shape and cut each rectangle into 4 triangles. Make a filling with the egg whites, stiffly beaten, 1/2 cup sugar, chopped nuts, and cinnamon. Spread a teaspoonful on each triangle and roll up, placing each butterhorn on buttered cookie sheet, seam-side down. Don't allow to rise. Bake at 350° for 15 to 18 minutes. Remove from oven; while still warm glaze with icing.

A Conversation with the Cook... "For an extra touch, use this thin icing with any of the fruit-bread recipes in this book, icing them while still warm."

✧

Peach Coffee Cake
Makes 8 servings

3/4 cup milk, heated to scalding (which is just before boiling)
1 package dry yeast
1/4 cup water
3 1/4 cups sifted all-purpose flour
2 eggs
1/2 cup soft butter
1/2 cup sugar
1/2 teaspoon salt
2 tablespoons melted butter
1 tablespoon sugar
3 cups sliced peaches
1 teaspoon cinnamon
1/8 teaspoon nutmeg
1/2 cup sugar

Scald milk; cool to lukewarm. Dissolve yeast in warm water. Add milk. Stir in 1 1/2 cups flour; beat until smooth. Cover; let rise until doubled, about 1 hour. Add eggs, one at a time, beating well after each. Stir in 1/2 cup soft butter, 1/2 cup sugar, salt, and remaining flour. Beat well. Spread dough in greased 9 x 9 x 2 - inch square baking pan. Spoon 2 tablespoons melted butter and 1 tablespoon sugar over dough. Cover; let rise until doubled. Press peach slices into dough. Mix together cinnamon, nutmeg, and 1/2 cup sugar. Sprinkle over fruit. Bake in 375° oven 40 to 45 minutes.

A Conversation with the Cook... "To easily peel peaches, dip in scalding water for 30 seconds, then plunge into ice water. Skins will peel right off."

Banana Chocolate-Chip Muffins

Makes 12 muffins

2 extra-ripe bananas
2 eggs
3/4 cup brown sugar
1/2 cup butter, melted
1 teaspoon vanilla
2 1/4 cups flour
2 teaspoons baking powder
1 teaspoon cinnamon
1 cup chocolate chips

Mash bananas. In large bowl, beat bananas, eggs, sugar, butter, and vanilla until blended. Add flour, baking powder, and cinnamon. Stir in chocolate chips. Mix just until blended. Spoon into paper-lined muffin tins. Bake at 350° for 25 to 30 minutes. Remove from pan and let cool.

A Conversation with the Cook... "For tender muffins, mix liquid and dry ingredients until just moistened. Over-mixing causes muffins to be tough, coarse-textured, and full of tunnels."

*"Nine out of ten people like chocolate.
The tenth person always lies."
~John J. Tullius, American cartoonist*

Dottie's Blueberry Muffins
Makes 1 dozen

Batter:
1/2 cup sugar
1/4 cup butter
1 egg
2 1/2 cups cake flour, sifted
4 teaspoons baking powder
1/4 teaspoon salt
1 cup milk
1 teaspoon vanilla
1 1/2 cups blueberries

Crumble Topping:
1/2 cup sugar
1 teaspoon cinnamon
2/3 cup flour
1/4 cup butter

In mixing bowl, cream sugar and butter until fluffy. Beat in egg. In separate bowl, combine flour, baking powder, and salt. Add dry ingredients to sugar and egg mixture, alternating with milk, beginning and ending with flour mixture. Add vanilla; beat well. Gently fold in blueberries. Spoon mixture into paper-lined muffin cups. Mix topping and sprinkle on top of each muffin. Bake muffins at 375° for 20 to 25 minutes or until golden brown.

A Conversation with the Cook about Flour and Mixing... "Most recipes call for all-purpose flour or just the word 'flour.' But there are many other flours out there, such as: cake flour, un-bleached flour, self-rising flour, rice flour, whole wheat flour, potato flour, masa harina, gluten flour, etc., etc.

Your recipe will have special adjustments built into its directions for the specific flour called for. For best results use the type of flour listed in the recipe, although substitutions can be made in a pinch. (Look these up on the internet, or in a definitive cookbook.)

Sift the flour with any dry ingredients called for in the recipe (such as salt, baking powder, etc.) and add to recipe as specified (for example: 1/3 at a time, alternating with _____ and blending well each addition, etc.). The pre-sifting of the dry ingredients and the gradual mixing of wet/and dry together will evenly distribute all ingredients to make for a more thoroughly mixed batter and optimum baking results.

You'll also notice it is important not to over-mix your batters—as this can lead to tough results. A delicate hand is a pre-requisite when baking. With a little practice, you'll be like my grandmother, Dottie ... a real pro."

"Aromatherapy for the Kitchen"

1/2 small can whole allspice
1/2 small can whole cloves
1/2 can stick cinnamon
2 or 3 star anise
Rind of a small orange
1 or 2 cups water

Simmer in open pan on stove top during the holidays.

A Conversation with the Cooks ..."Makes a wonderful festive yet soothing aroma to filter through the house. Do not leave simmering potpourri unattended, anymore than you would a burning candle."

Dorothy's Special Strawberry Muffins

Makes 6 large muffins

1 cup flour
1/3 cup sugar
1/4 teaspoon baking soda
1/4 teaspoon baking powder
1/4 teaspoon ginger
1 teaspoon cinnamon
1 egg
1/4 cup butter, melted
2 tablespoons water
2 tablespoons lemon juice
1 cup strawberries, sliced

Sift flour with sugar, baking soda, baking powder, ginger, and cinnamon; set aside. In separate bowl, beat egg, butter, water, and lemon juice. Add flour mixture and the sliced strawberries all at once to egg mixture; stir just until mixed. Pour into 6 paper-lined muffin cups. (Don't forget to grease top of muffin tin.) Bake at 400° until golden, about 25 minutes.

A Conversation with the Cook... "My Mother's favorite was anything with strawberries in it, so here's to you Mom!"

> *"Strawberries are a member of the rose family and are the only fruit that have their seeds on the outside."*
> *~a bit of trivia*

Sweet Potato Biscuits

Makes 12 servings

2 cups flour
1/4 cup sugar
4 teaspoons baking powder
1/4 teaspoon salt
1 teaspoon cinnamon
1/2 teaspoon nutmeg
1/2 cup butter
1/2 cup chopped pecans
2/3 cup cooked mashed sweet potato
1/3 cup evaporated milk

Cook sweet potatoes in salted water. Drain and mash. Set aside. Sift together flour, sugar, baking powder, salt, cinnamon, and nutmeg. Cut butter into flour mixture until it crumbles. Stir in pecans. Combine sweet potatoes and evaporated milk. Stir into flour mixture. Dough should be stiff. Turn onto floured board. Knead several times on floured surface. Pat into 1/2-inch thickness. Cut out with 2-inch round biscuit-cutter. Place biscuits on lightly greased baking sheet. Bake at 400° for 12 to 15 minutes.

A Conversation with the Cook... "Serve these melt-in-your-mouth biscuits warm with any dinner and listen to the rave reviews roll in ... better make a double batch!"

Carrot and Pineapple Muffins

Makes 24 small or 12 large muffins

2 1/3 cups flour
2 teaspoons baking powder
1 1/2 teaspoon baking soda
2 1/2 teaspoons cinnamon
1/2 teaspoon salt
1/8 teaspoon nutmeg
1/8 teaspoon cloves
1/8 teaspoon allspice
1 cup sugar
1/4 cup olive oil
1/2 cup sour cream
3 eggs
2 cups carrots, grated
1 (8 ounce) can crushed pineapple, well drained

Spray muffin cups with Pam® or use paper liners. Sift together flour, baking powder, baking soda, cinnamon, salt, nutmeg, cloves, and allspice into a large bowl; set aside. In mixing bowl, combine sugar, oil, sour cream, and eggs; beat until smooth. Add carrots and pineapple. Fold in dry ingredients, mixing just until moistened. Spoon batter into muffin cups and bake for 15 to 20 minutes at 425°, or until muffins test done with a toothpick.

A Conversation with the Cook... "If angels could invent a muffin recipe, this would be it."

Sour Cream Coffeecake

Makes 12 servings

3/4 cup sugar
2 teaspoons cinnamon
1/2 cup walnuts, chopped
2 cups flour
1/2 teaspoon baking powder
1/2 teaspoon baking soda
1/4 teaspoon salt
1 cup sugar
1/2 cup butter
2 eggs
1 cup cultured sour cream

Combine first 3 ingredients; set aside. Cream butter and sugar at medium speed; add eggs, one at a time, mixing each addition. Sift together dry ingredients and add, alternately with sour cream. Pour 1/2 batter into greased and floured Bundt™ pan. Sprinkle with 1/2 of the cinnamon/nut mixture; add remaining batter. Sprinkle rest of cinnamon/nut mixture over top. Bake at 350° for about 35 minutes, or until toothpick in center comes out clean. Cool before un-molding.

A Conversation with the Cook... "A classic recipe, this makes a wonderful Sunday Morning Brunch cake or a lazy-day breakfast over coffee and the newspaper."

Fresh Pretzels
Makes 8 servings

Put into a large bowl and stir until dissolved:
  1 1/4 teaspoons dry yeast
  3/4 cup warm water

Sift into small bowl:
  1 1/2 cups flour
  1 teaspoon sugar
  1/2 teaspoon salt

Gradually add the flour mixture to the liquid mixture. Use your hands and work dough until it's soft and firm but not sticky. Add a little more flour if necessary, about 1 tablespoon. Knead dough until smooth and elastic about 5 minutes. Grease a medium size bowl. Lightly grease your fingertips and place the dough in the bowl. Set aside.

At time of baking:
  1 egg, beaten
  Coarse salt

Grease a cookie sheet. Divide dough into 15 pieces. With your hands, roll each piece from center out to ends, forming a thin rope about a foot long. Loop each rope into the shape of a pretzel and place on cookie sheet. Brush each pretzel with beaten egg; sprinkle with coarse salt. Bake 10 to 15 minutes in 450° oven, until golden brown.

A Conversation with the Cook... "These pretzels are for you, Brook."

*"There is one thing more exasperating
than a wife who can cook and won't
and that's a wife who can't cook and will."
~ Robert Frost*

Old Fashioned Corn Biscuits
Makes 6 servings

1 3/8 cups flour
5/8 cup cornmeal
2 tablespoons sugar
2 teaspoons baking powder
1/2 teaspoon salt
1 egg
3/4 cup sour cream
1/2 teaspoon baking soda

First sift flour, cornmeal, sugar, baking powder, and salt together. Secondly beat the egg, and add sour cream and baking soda. Stir both mixtures together only until mixed. Turn out on floured board; knead slightly to 3/4-inch thickness. Cut with biscuit cutter. Place on greased baking sheet. Bake at 450° for 15 minutes. Serve hot.

A Conversation with the Cook... "Kneading the dough for a half minute after mixing improves the texture of the biscuits."

"To give life to beauty the painter uses a whole range of colors, the musician uses sounds, and the cook bakes biscuits."
~adapted from a thought by Lucien Tendret

Big Apple Pancake
Makes 6 servings

6 egg yolks
6 egg whites, stiffly beaten
1/4 cup flour
1/4 cup melted butter
2 tablespoons butter
1/4 cup milk
1/4 teaspoon salt
3 apples, peeled, cored, and sliced
1/2 cup sugar
1 tablespoon cinnamon

Beat eggs yolks; mix in flour, melted butter, milk, and salt. Fold in the beaten egg whites. Heat 2 tablespoons butter in a large oven proof (preferably cast-iron) skillet; pour in batter. Top with apple slices. Cook over medium heat for about 5 minutes. Transfer skillet from stove top to oven. Bake in 400° oven for 15 minutes until golden brown. Mix sugar and cinnamon and sprinkle over top of pancake. Cut into wedges to serve.

A Conversation with the Cook... "2-step cooking (stove top and baking) in a heavy skillet adds much flavor to this unique pancake. My mother's old cast iron skillet works perfectly for this recipe."

A Note about Cast Iron Cookware... "Some extra attention is needed for cast iron cookware. If you have a new cast iron skillet it must be 'seasoned' before you use it. Rub down its interior with a thin coating of

Crisco® and bake in a 350° oven for 1 hour. Remove from oven and cool. Rub down with a paper towel and store the pan away with out washing. Whenever pan begins to look 'dry' 'season' it again in this manner and your cast iron skillet will last you many years. For some recipes you just can't beat your trusty cast-iron skillet

✧

Irish Oatmeal Bread
Makes 2 loaves

2 cups cooked oatmeal
1/2 teaspoon salt
1 tablespoon sugar
1 tablespoon shortening
5 teaspoons baking powder
1 egg, beaten
1/2 cup milk
3 1/2 cups flour

Add salt, sugar, and shortening to oatmeal; set aside. Sift flour and baking powder together; set aside. Add egg and milk to oatmeal mixture. Then work in the flour mixture. Mix and knead for 5 minutes. Place in greased loaf pans and bake for 1 hour at 375°. Serve with Honey Butter (see page 262).

A Conversation with the Cook... "Over-kneading may cause large air holes in the crust.

Cereal Coffee Cake
Makes 9 to 12 servings

Batter:
1 3/4 cups flour
1 cup sugar
3 teaspoons baking powder
1/2 teaspoon salt
1/3 cup butter, softened
1 egg
1 cup milk
1 1/2 cups Total® breakfast cereal

Crunchy Topping:
2 tablespoons firm butter
1/4 cup brown sugar, packed
2 tablespoons flour
2 teaspoons cinnamon

Mix all batter ingredients except cereal; beat 2 minutes. Fold in cereal. Spread batter in greased baking pan, 9 x 9 x 2-inches. Mix topping ingredients until crumbly and sprinkle over batter. Bake 35 to 40 minutes in 350° oven. Serve warm or cooled, it's delightful either way.

A Conversation with the Cook... "For a 'sin-cereal-y' good breakfast experience, make yourself a good cup of coffee, a glass of juice or a plate of fresh fruit, and a wedge of this coffee cake for a 'total-y' great way to start your day."

Chapter Nine
Sweet Nothings
That are Everything ...
In Other Words, Dessert

✧

"A good meal deserves a good dessert."
~MaryAnn

RECIPE INDEX

Aunt Louise's Formula for Pie Crust ... 297
Cranberry Apple Pie ... 299
Summer Peach Parfait Pie ... 300
Easy and Elegant Summer Fruit Pie ... 301
Gail's Chocolate Pie Divine ... 302
Southern Chess Pie ... 303
Peggy's Prune Pie ... 304
Lucile's Pineapple Cheese Pie ... 305
Linda's Pineapple Cream Pie ... 305
Cream Puff Pastry ... 306
Margarite's Pineapple Upside Down Cake ... 307
Auntie's Pear & Cranberry Upside Down Cake ... 309
Peggy's Plum Cake ... 310
Mother's Old Fashioned Bread Pudding ... 312
Sour Cream Cake ... 313

Poppy Seed Pound Cake ... 315
"Next Day" Meringue Shells ... 316
Chocolate Mint Brownies ... 317
Chocolate Chocolate-Chip Zucchini Cake ... 319
Creamy Apple Dessert ... 320
Honey Cake ... 321
Rich Devil's Food Cake ... 323
Butterscotch Cake 324
Fruit Cocktail Cake ... 327
Strawberry Cake ... 328
Rhubarb Special ... 330
Rhubarb Crunch ... 332
Angel's 3-Layer Lemon Cake ... 333
Rice Krispies® Cookies ... 334
Coconut-Oatmeal Cookies ... 336
Banana Chip Bars ... 337
Dottie's Danish Sugar Cookies ... 338
Trick or Treat Monster Cookies ... 339
Mother's Almond Crescents ... 340
Gingerbread-Currant Cakes-in-a-Jar ... 341

Aunt Louise's Formula for Pie Crust

Use a ratio of:
2 parts flour
1 part lard
Pinch of salt
Several tablespoons of ice-water (to be added 1 tablespoon at a time)

(Use approximately 2 cups flour, 1 cup lard, and 4 or 5 tablespoons water for double-crust pie)

✧

(Use approximately 1 cup flour, 1/2 cup lard, and 3-or-so tablespoons water for single-crust pie)

With a table fork or wire-pastry blender, blend flour and lard to small crumbs. Add ice water 1 tablespoon at a time, until you get a smooth (but not sticky) dough that can be rolled out into crust. (I like to use a floured cloth surface and a floured "mitten-ed" rollingpin for rolling out my crust. You can find this old fashioned cloth-set at old fashioned hardware stores or gourmet outfitters.) Work quickly, on your floured surface, rolling out your crust for a one-crust, or double-crust pie. Do not over-work as pie crust will become tough. To transfer crust to pie plate, gently roll it around your rolling pin and un-roll into the pie plate. Make it large enough so dough hangs over the edge—as you will "crimp" (or pinch) this up to form a decorative rim to hold in your filling (in the case of a single-crust pie), or to seal top and bottom crusts together (for a double-crust pie).

A Conversation with the Cook... "I pride myself in making the flakiest, almost-too-tender pie crust around ... I learned from the best, my namesake, Aunt Louise. I cannot bake a loaf of yeast bread, but I **can** make pie crust.

Rule#1: you must use lard (you can find this next to the yeast in your market's dairy counter section).

Rule#2: you must use ice-cold, ice water.

Rule#3: work quickly, and do not over-work your dough.

Rule#4: if you feel at all intimidated, just buy pre-made crusts and proceed from there—after all it's the filling that is going to be the most prominent star of the pie. I won't tell, if you won't."

Cranberry Apple Pie

Makes 1 (8 or 9-inch) double crust, lattice-topped pie

1 cup sugar
1/4 cup tapioca
1 1/2 teaspoons grated orange peel
1/4 teaspoon salt
4 to 5 medium apples, peeled, cored, and sliced
1 cup raw cranberries
Dots of butter
Crusts for a 2-crust pie

Toss first 6 ingredients to mix and make a filling. Mound filling into bottom pie crust. Dot with butter. Cut top crust into long strips and weave in lattice fashion over top of filling. Crimp edges. Bake at 425° until bubbly, about 50 minutes. Serve warm, "al a mode" with vanilla ice cream.

A Conversation with the Cook... "This is such a pretty pie and tastes even better the next day."

"Thy breath is like the steame of apple-pyes."
~Robert Greene, the year was 1590,
the reference surely a beautiful woman

Summer Peach Parfait Pie

Makes 1 (9 -inch) single crust pie

3 1/2 cups sliced fresh peaches, sweetened with a little sugar (or use 1 {2 1/2 pound} can peach slices, drained, but reserving juice)
Water
1 (3 ounce) package lemon Jell-O®
1/2 cup cold water
1 pint vanilla ice cream
1 baked (9 -inch) pie shell
Whipped cream

Peel and slice fresh peaches into a bowl, sprinkle with sugar, and let stand 15 minutes. Drain peaches, reserving sugared juice. Add water to this juice to make 1 cup (if you are using canned peaches, reserve that juice.). Heat to boiling, and add the jell-O® to dissolve. Add 1/2 cup cold water to cool down the mixture. Cut ice cream into 6 pieces and stir into the hot liquid. Chill mixture until it mounds slightly. Fold in the sweetened peaches and pour filling into baked pie shell that has cooled. Chill several hours, until set. Top with whipped cream at time of serving. Can slice an additional fresh peach for garnish.

A Conversation with the Cook... "When we were building our first house, I used to make lunch for the carpenters. This pie was their favorite and I almost think they would have worked for free, just to get this pie."

Easy and Elegant Summer Fruit Pie

Makes 1 single-crust pie

1 baked and cooled pie shell
1 pint whipping cream, whipped stiff
Fresh raspberries, or blueberries, or strawberries (hulled and left whole), or peach slices (select one fruit per pie)
1/4 cup red currant jelly
1 to 2 tablespoons water

Bake pie shell and cool. Whip cream stiff and spread evenly into pie shell. Gently top with fruit of choice, in a single layer to completely cover the whipped cream. (If using strawberries, arrange them side by side, pointy-side-up like little mountains.) Refrigerate. In a small saucepan melt the currant jelly and water to make a glaze. Cool just slightly. Remove pie from refrigerator and drizzle glaze over berries, to completely coat and glaze. Return pie to refrigerator until serving time.

A Conversation with the Cook... "This is one of the most fabulous and 'showy' ways I have found to serve summer fruit. The red currant glaze just makes the pie! Everyone always wants the recipe."

Gail's Chocolate Pie Divine
Makes 1 (10-inch) meringue-crust pie

4 egg whites
1/4 teaspoon cream of tartar
1 cup sugar
6 ounces chocolate chips
Dash cinnamon
4 egg yolks, beaten
1 teaspoon vanilla
1 cup heavy cream, whipped and sweetened
Additional whipped cream and chocolate curls, for garnish

Make a "meringue-crust" by beating egg whites stiff, but not dry. Add cream of tartar and sugar, and continue beating until glossy. Spread meringue into a 10-nch pie plate, making high sides around the edge. Bake "meringue shell" at 300° for 1 hour. Meanwhile, melt the chocolate and cinnamon in a double boiler. Cool slightly and beat in the egg yolks and vanilla. Fold in the cup of heavy whipped cream to blend. Pour filling into the cooled meringue shell. Garnish with more whipped cream and a sprinkling of chocolate curls. (To make chocolate curls, simply run a potato peeler down the side of a chocolate candy bar, or a block of baking chocolate that has been chilled just slightly.) After garnishing pie chill in refrigerator until serving.

A Conversation with the Cook... "I'm tempted to rename this Cloud Nine Pie ... it's that good."

Southern Chess Pie

Makes 1 (9-inch) single crust pie

Pastry for a 1 crust pie (or use ready made pie shell)
1 cup brown sugar, packed
1/2 cup white sugar
1 tablespoon flour
2 eggs
2 tablespoons milk
1 teaspoon vanilla
1/2 cup butter, melted
1 cup chopped pecans
Rich vanilla ice cream, at serving time

To make filling, mix brown sugar, white sugar, and flour together. Beat in thoroughly: eggs, milk, vanilla, and butter in that order. Fold in nuts. Pour filling into crust. Bake at 375° for 40 to 50 minutes. Serve small pieces warm (this pie is very rich) with rich vanilla ice cream. (I like to use Edie's® Homemade-style Custard Ice Cream.)

A Conversation with the Cook... "You'd better make two of these, 'cuz they won't last long. This pie is so (almost tooth-achingly) sweet, I like to 'cut it' with a little ice cream. This pie keeps well and tastes great the next day."

Peggy's Prune Pie
Makes 1 (9-inch) single crust pie

1 (9-inch) unbaked pie shell
3 eggs, beaten
4 tablespoons flour
1 cup sugar
Pinch salt
Dash cinnamon
1 cup milk
1/2 cup prune juice
1 teaspoon vanilla
1 cup diced cooked prunes
Whipped cream, at serving time

Mix together beaten eggs, flour, sugar, salt, and cinnamon. Stir in milk, prune juice, vanilla, and diced prunes. Pour filling into pie shell. Bake at 375° for 50 to 60 minutes, or until set and knife inserted in center comes out clean. Top servings with whipped cream.

A Conversation with the Cook... "I have always loved prunes. (My mother made great prune desserts, but unfortunately so many jokes have been made about prunes, that they have become a rather ignored sweet.) Try this pie, and I think you just might be sold on prunes once in a while."

"One of the best investments you'll ever make is feeding your family well."
~Wendy Louise

Lucile's Pineapple Cheese Pie
Makes 1 (9-inch) graham cracker crust pie

1 (9-inch) graham cracker pie shell, baked and cooled according to package instructions
1 (8 ounce) package cream cheese, at room temperature
1/4 cup sugar
1 cup heavy cream, whipped
1 1/2 cups crushed pineapple (taken from a 1 pound 4 ounce can) drained very well

Bake and cool graham pie shell. Set aside. To make filling, whip together cream cheese and sugar blending well. Fold in the whipped cream. Fold in the drained pineapple. Spoon mixture into graham shell. Chill for at least 2 hours before serving.

Linda's Pineapple Cream Pie
Makes 1 (9-inch) graham cracker crust pie

1 baked and cooled (9-inch) graham cracker pie shell
1 can crushed pineapple
1 large container sour cream
1 small box instant vanilla pudding

Mix together pineapple, sour cream, and instant pudding. Pour into cooked graham cracker pie shell. Chill for at least 2 hours before serving.

A Conversation with the Cook... "Two cooks, two versions, you choose your favorite."

Cream Puff Pastry

1 cup water
1/2 cup butter
1 cup flour
1/4 teaspoon salt
4 eggs

Bring water and butter to a boil. Add flour and salt all at once. Lower heat. Stir until mixture forms a ball. Cool slightly. Add eggs one at a time, beating till smooth and shiny.

For miniature puffs, drop dough by teaspoonfuls on un-greased cookie sheet. Bake at 375° for 35 minutes.

For standard-size puffs, drop dough by heaping table-spoonfuls, 3-inches apart on un-greased cookie sheets. Bake at 450° for 15 minutes, drop oven setting to 325° and bake 25 minutes more. Remove puffs from oven and slice puffs in half. Turn off oven. Return puffs to warm oven for 20 minutes to dry out their interiors.

A Conversation with the Cook... "Your puffs are now ready to fill, using anything from whipped cream for dessert puffs to chicken salad for luncheon puffs. Miniature ones make great finger-food appetizers (see Avocado Puffs page 16)."

Margarite's Pineapple Upside Down Cake

Makes 1 (approximately 12-inch) round single layer cake, about 8 to 10 servings

Glazed fruit layer:
A heavy, old-fashioned cast-iron skillet
1/4 cup butter, melted
1 cup brown sugar
Canned pineapple slices, drain and retain juice
Maraschino cherries
Chopped walnuts (optional)

Coat the bottom of a heavy, oven-safe pan (an old cast iron skillet is best) with the melted butter. Sprinkle in the brown sugar evenly around the pan. Lay in the pineapple slices. Put a cherry in center of each slice, Sprinkle on some chopped walnuts if desired. Set aside while you mix the batter.

Cake batter:
1 1/4 cup flour
1/2 cup sugar
2 teaspoons baking powder
1/2 teaspoon salt
1/3 cup butter, melted
7 tablespoons pineapple juice (from the drained pineapple)
1 egg

Mix dry ingredients together. Mix in melted butter, then pineapple juice, then egg. Beat 2 minutes. Pour cake batter evenly over pineapple-glaze in the skillet.

Place in 375° oven and bake for 45 minutes. When cake is done let cool for 5 or so minutes before inverting onto serving plate. Can serve topped with whipped cream, or even ice cream.

A Conversation with the Cook... "A recipe as old as my inherited cast iron skillet, yet as delectable today as when my mother used to make it. See page 291 for information on caring for cast iron."

Auntie's Pear and Cranberry Upside Down Cake

Makes 1 single layer cake, about 6 to 8 servings

Glazed fruit layer:
1 cup, cranberries, fresh or frozen, cooked 5 minutes and drained
1 can halved pears, drained, but reserve juice
2 tablespoons melted butter
1/2 cup brown sugar

Prepare fruit, butter, and sugar and arrange attractively in bottom of casserole dish, 8-inch square Pyrex® baking dish, or cast iron skillet. Set aside.

Cake batter:
1 1/2 cups flour
2 1/2 teaspoons baking powder
1/3 cup softened butter creamed together with
3/4 cup sugar, mixing well
1 teaspoon vanilla
1 egg
1/3 cup reserved pear juice

Make a cake batter by mixing together ingredients in order listed. Mix well and spread over the arranged fruit. Bake at 350° for 40 minutes. Remove from oven and let cake cool for 5 minutes before inverting onto serving plate.

A Conversation with the Cook... "Serve up wedges, warm or cool, with a topping of whipped cream."

Peggy's Plum Cake

Makes 1 (8 x 8-inch) single layer crumble-cake, about 9 servings

For Dough:
1 cup flour
1 teaspoon baking powder
1/4 cup sugar
1 tablespoon Crisco®
1 tablespoon butter

For Top:
9 to 12 blue plums, halved and pitted

For Crumble Topping:
3/4 cup sugar
1 teaspoon cinnamon
1 tablespoon butter
1 tablespoon flour

At Serving Time:
Whipped cream

Mix flour, baking powder, and 1/4 cup sugar together. Blend in the Crisco® and butter to make crumbly dough. Pat dough into a well-greased 8 x 8-inch square pan, making sides slightly raised (so plums won't burn and stick to sides of pan). Arrange the halved plums over the dough, but not touching sides of pan. Combine the 4 crumble-topping ingredients and sprinkle over the plums. Start by baking at 400° for 10 minutes; reduce to 300° and bake 40 minutes more. When done, cover top with another pan (or foil) and bake covered just a few minutes more to form a glaze on the top of the cake. Remove from oven, and remove foil top, set on wrack to cool. Serve with whipped cream.

A Conversation with the Cook... "Another one of my favorites— Peggy reached perfection with this one!"

"Dinner is like a short story,
the dessert the happy ending."
~Wendy Louise

Mother's Old Fashioned Bread Pudding

Makes 6 to 8 servings

2 cups milk
1/4 cup butter
4 cups coarse bread crumbs (cubed day old bread)
1/2 cup sugar
1/4 teaspoon salt
1 cup raisins
3/4 teaspoon cinnamon
1/4 teaspoon nutmeg
2 eggs, slightly beaten
Half-and-half cream, at serving time

Heat milk and butter to scalding and pour over bread crumbs. Mix in remaining ingredients (except half-and-half). Pour into a buttered 1 1/2-quart casserole. Bake at 350° for 40 to 45 minutes, or until knife pierced in center comes out clean. Serve warm with whipped cream, vanilla ice cream, or as my mother used to do—put each warm-from-the-oven serving in a dish and pass half-and-half cream to pour over.

A Conversation with the Cook... "Hmm, hmm, hmm...this is a great way to use up leftover bread. I've used everything from hot dog buns, to French bread, to raisin bread, to whole wheat—each makes a great taste all its own. Put in the oven just as you sit down for dinner and you'll have a straight-out-of-the-oven dessert to finish off your meal."

Sour Cream Cake
Makes 10 servings

2 sticks soft butter
1 1/2 cups sugar
3 eggs
1 1/2 teaspoons vanilla
2 1/2 cups unbleached flour
2 1/2 teaspoons baking powder
1/2 teaspoon baking soda
1/2 teaspoon salt
1 cup sour cream
1/2 cup chopped pecans
2 teaspoons cinnamon
1/4 cup additional sugar
Sifted confectioners' sugar, at serving time

Beat butter for 3 minutes. Add sugar and beat 3 more minutes. Add eggs 1 at a time, beating well each addition. Add vanilla; set aside. In separate bowl, mix together flour, baking powder, baking soda, and salt. Now add half of the flour mixture, then sour cream, then remaining flour mixture into the egg mixture, beating all the while. Put half of the batter mixture into a buttered and floured Bundt-style cake pan. In a little bowl, mix together the pecans, cinnamon, and additional sugar. Sprinkle half of this nut mixture on the cake layer. Pour on remaining batter. Sprinkle on remaining nut mixture. Bake at 325° for 1 hour. Cool slightly before inverting onto cake plate. Dust with confectioners' sugar just before serving, by tapping the sugar through a sieve onto the cooled cake.

A Conversation with the Cook... "Rich and mellow...who says all things need to be chocolate! Bundt™ cake pans can be found at cooking specialty stores, and are great for baking rich, dense cakes, such as pound cake and this cake. A good Bundt-style pan is heavy and I like a Teflon® lined one. The pan gives the cake a decorative, ring-mold pattern and is easy to un-mold."

Poppy Seed Pound Cake
Makes 10 servings

1 package yellow layer cake mix
1 (3 ounce) package vanilla instant pudding
1/2 cup vegetable oil
4 eggs
1 cup water
1/4 cup poppy seeds
Powdered sugar, at time of serving

Blend all and beat 2 minutes. Pour into 10-inch greased and floured tube pan or Bundt™ pan. Bake at 350° for 45 to 55 minutes. When cooled, invert on cake plate and dust with powdered sugar, shaken through a sieve.

A Conversation with the Cook... "This makes a great brunch or luncheon cake, when you don't want something too heavy or too sweet."

"Never eat more than you can lift"
~Miss Piggy

"Next Day" Meringue Shells
Makes 12

6 egg whites
1/2 teaspoon cream of tartar
2 cups sugar

Beat egg whites with cream of tartar until frothy. Gradually beat in sugar, adding a little at a time, beating till stiff and glossy. Line a baking sheet with brown paper or parchment cooking paper. Mound meringue onto paper and press a "well" into each meringue with the back of a spoon. Put in 400° oven, turn off heat, and walk away. Let meringues stand overnight in oven—do NOT open oven door, do NOT peek. Next day remove shells from oven and store on kitchen counter. At time of serving, fill meringues with vanilla ice cream and top with a summer fruit, such as sliced strawberries for what is known as Schaum Torte. Or fill with coffee ice cream and top with chocolate sauce.

A Conversation with the Cook... "Now you know the secret for how to make fool-proof meringues! See how many different fillings you can come up with to vary the dessert."

> *"Seize the moment.*
> *Remember all those women on the Titanic*
> *who waved off the dessert cart."*
> *~ Erma Bombeck*

Chocolate Mint Brownies
Makes 24 bars

First layer:
1/2 cup butter, melted
1 cup sugar
4 eggs
1/2 teaspoon baking powder
1 cup flour
1 (16 ounce) can Hershey® chocolate syrup

In large bowl combine above ingredients, beat until smooth. Put in a greased and floured cookie sheet with sides. Bake at 350° for 20 minutes. Cool 10 minutes.

Second layer:
1/2 cup butter
2 cups powdered sugar
2 tablespoons milk
1 teaspoon peppermint extract
Few drops green food coloring

Mix all ingredients. Spread over 1st layer. Refrigerate for 20 minutes.

Third layer:
1/2 cup butter
1 cup chocolate chips

Gently melt butter and chocolate chips in a small pan. Then spread over 2nd layer. Refrigerate 5 minutes and cut into bars.

A Conversation with the Cook... "When you are asked to 'bring' a dessert—this is it! No one can resist these."

Chocolate Chocolate-Chip Zucchini Cake

Makes 12 servings

1/2 cup olive oil
2 cups grated zucchini
1/3 cup butter, at room temperature
1 3/4 cups sugar
2 eggs
1/2 teaspoon vanilla
1/2 cup sour milk (see page 264 on how to sour milk)
2 1/2 cups flour
1/2 teaspoon baking powder
1 teaspoon cinnamon
1/4 cup cocoa
1 teaspoon baking soda
1/4 cup chocolate chips, at baking time

Blend oil and zucchini; set aside. In large bowl cream butter and sugar; fold in zucchini mixture and eggs. *Set aside. In second bowl* add vanilla to sour milk. In separate bowl sift together all dry ingredients, except chocolate chips. Add milk alternately with dry ingredients to zucchini/egg mixture, blending well each addition. Grease 13 x 9-inch pan. Spread mixture in pan and cover with chocolate chips before baking. Bake at 350° for 40 minutes. Cool before serving.

A Conversation with the Cook... "When you are creaming butter and sugar together, it's a good idea to rinse the bowl with boiling water first. They'll cream faster."

Creamy Apple Dessert

Makes 6 servings

1/4 cup butter
1 1/2 cups graham cracker crumbs
1 (14 ounce) can sweetened condensed milk
1 cup sour cream
1/4 cup lemon juice
1 (21 ounce) can apple pie filling
1/4 cup chopped walnuts
1 teaspoon cinnamon

In 10 x 6-inch baking dish, place butter and melt in pre-heated oven. Remove dish from oven and stir graham cracker crumbs into butter until well mixed. Press and pat on bottom and up sides of baking dish to coat; set aside. In medium bowl, mix together condensed milk, sour cream, and lemon juice. Spread creamy mixture evenly over crumbs. Spoon canned apple pie filling over creamy layer. Bake 25 to 30 minutes at 350° until set. Let cool. In small dish, mix nuts and cinnamon, sprinkle over top before serving. Serve cold or room temperature. Refrigerate leftovers.

A Conversation with the Cook... "The clue in this recipe is to be sure to let the dessert cool before you do the last step. Terrific dessert for the beginner cook."

Honey Cake

Makes 12 servings

Cake:
1/3 cup shortening
1/2 cup honey
1/2 cup sugar
2 eggs, well beaten
1/2 cup milk
1 3/4 cups flour
1/2 teaspoon salt
2 teaspoons baking powder
1 teaspoon cinnamon
1/2 teaspoon ginger
1/4 teaspoon cloves

Cream shortening with honey and sugar till very light. Add eggs and beat them in well. Sift flour with all dry ingredients and add alternately with the milk to the egg mixture, mixing well each addition. Pour into 2 well greased 8-inch pans. Bake for 30 minutes at 350°. Cool completely before frosting with the recipe that follows.

Frosting for Honey Cake:
16 ounces cream cheese, at room temperature
2 tablespoons milk
1 teaspoon vanilla extract
1/3 cup honey

With electric mixer, soften and blend together cream cheese, milk, and vanilla extract, whipping until smooth. Drizzle in the honey, mixing all the while, until you arrive at a smooth and spread-able consistency. Add more milk as/and if necessary, 1 tablespoon at a time to thin frosting. Carefully frost cake, taking care not to tear the cake. *Note: Sometimes when I'm frosting a cake, I like to dip my spatula or knife into hot water, before dipping into the frosting. This makes the frosting easier to spread.*

A Conversation with the Cook... "I have to tell you a story about making my first batch of cookies (before moving on to cake). I was 10 years old when I made my first attempt. My Mom said it was okay for me to give it a try so I started with a cookie recipe called Honey Cookies. I began putting together the ingredients without looking to see if I even had them all—and low and behold we didn't have any honey, for my honey cookies! So I thought well as long as I am this far why not try making them anyway. So I baked up my batch of tasteless cookies and my family has teased me about my baking skills (be it all in good fun) ever since—so moral of the story—read your recipe through and gather all your ingredients before you start!"

> *"The only reason for being a bee that I know of is making honey ... And the only reason for making honey is so I can eat it."*
> *~Winnie the Pooh*

Rich Devil's Food Cake
Makes 12 servings

1/2 cup butter, softened
2 cups light brown sugar, packed
2 eggs
2 1/4 cups cake flour
1/4 teaspoon salt
1/2 cup sour milk (see page 264)
1 teaspoon baking soda
1 teaspoon vanilla
1/2 cup boiling water
1 1/2 squares sweet chocolate, melted

Mix first 8 ingredients together to make a thoroughly mixed batter. Mix hot water and melted chocolate together and then add to batter. Pour into 13 x 9-inch greased and floured pan. Bake at 350° for 30 minutes.

A Conversation with the Cook... "Add a simple creamy vanilla frosting to top off the cake."

Simple Vanilla Frosting
1/3 cup butter, softened
3 cups sifted powdered sugar
1 teaspoon vanilla extract
2 1/2 to 3 tablespoons half-and-half, or whole milk

Cream butter and sugar. Stir in vanilla. Then blend in cream until spreading consistency is reached. Spread with spatula over cooled cake.

A Conversation with the Cook... "For a 'devilish' treat, 'brown' the butter before mixing as above, by gently heating in a skillet until deeply golden brown—but not burned. Browned Butter Frosting makes an uncommonly exquisite touch and you will receive many compliments for the unusual frosting."

"Man the life boats!
First the women and children; then the dessert cart!"
~Wendy Louise and MaryAnn,
agreeing with Erma Bombeck

Butterscotch Cake

Makes 12 servings

Cake:
6 egg yolks, beaten
1 1/2 cups sugar
1 teaspoon baking powder
2 teaspoons vanilla
6 egg whites, beaten stiff
2 cups graham crackers, crushed
1 cup nuts, chopped

Beat egg yolks, sugar, and baking powder. Add vanilla. Beat 6 egg whites stiff but not dry. Fold into yolk mixture. Add 2 cups graham crackers and 1 cup nuts. Pour into greased 13 x 9-inch pan and bake at 325° for 30 to 35 minutes. Cool cake before glazing.

Glaze:
1 cup brown sugar, packed
1 tablespoon flour
1/4 cup orange juice
1/4 cup butter
1/4 cup water
1 egg, beaten
1 teaspoon vanilla

For glaze cook over low heat, slowly bringing to a boil and blending all the while. Cool slightly before glazing cake.

Topping:
2 cups Cool Whip®

At time of serving spread with Cool Whip®.

A Conversation with the Cook... "This old fashioned recipe comes straight out of my mother's recipe box ... hmm, hmm, good. I make it today as she did then, and my granddaughters love it!"

Fruit Cocktail Cake
Makes 12 servings

Cake:
1 cup flour plus 2 tablespoons
1 cup sugar
1 teaspoon salt
1 teaspoon baking soda
1 teaspoon baking powder
1 (24 ounce) can fruit cocktail, drained of 1/2 the juice
1 egg

Topping:
1/2 cup brown sugar, packed
1/2 cup nuts, chopped

Mix dry ingredients well. Beat egg and add to dry mixture. Add fruit cocktail; which has 1/2 of juice drained. Mixture will be quite thin compared to other cakes. Put in greased 13 x 9-inch pan. Top with 1/2 cup brown sugar and 1/2 cup nuts. Bake at 350° for 30 to 35 minutes.

A Conversation with the Cook... "This cake can be served plain or topped with whipped topping. If you top it with ice cream that is called 'a la mode.'"

Strawberry Cake
Makes 12 servings

1 1/2 cups mini marshmallows
1/2 cup butter, softened
1 1/2 cups sugar
2 1/2 cups flour
3 teaspoons baking powder
1/4 teaspoon salt
1 cup milk
1 teaspoon vanilla
3 eggs
3 cups strawberries, sliced
1 (3 ounce) package strawberry gelatin, straight out of the package
Sweetened whipped cream, at time of serving

Grease 13 x 9-inch pan. Line bottom with marshmallows. Cream sugar and butter together in bowl; set aside. Mix flour with baking powder and salt; set aside. Mix milk with vanilla and eggs; set aside. Mix all mixtures together well and pour batter over marshmallows. Combine strawberries and dry gelatin. Spoon strawberry mixture evenly over cake. Bake at 350° for 45 to 50 minutes. Cool before serving. Top with whipped cream.

A Conversation with the Cook... "When whipping cream, make sure to chill your bowl and beaters, as well as having cold cream. Everything will mix quicker and easier. Sweeten the cream with 1 or 2 tablespoons confectioners' sugar or granulated sugar, while whipping."

"Let there be cake!"
~ a pronouncement by Marie Antionette,
who liked her cake
as much as Henry IV liked his chicken

Rhubarb Special

Makes 12 servings

Short Crust:
1/2 cup shortening
1/4 cup sugar
1 egg yolk
1 1/4 cup flour
Milk, as needed for crust

Cream well with shortening the sugar and egg yolk; mix in flour. Moisten with milk (like for pie crust) and roll out. Line a 13 x 9-inch pan.

Filling:
2 1/2 cups rhubarb
1/4 cup water

Mix together in sauce pan and bring to boil until rhubarb gets a little soft, then pour rhubarb into crust.

Custard:
1 egg white
2 eggs
1 1/4 cup sugar
Dash of salt
1/2 cup milk

Take the 1 egg white plus 2 whole eggs and beat well; add sugar, dash of salt, and milk. Mix well and pour over rhubarb in pie crust. Bake at 350° for 45 minutes. Serve with whipped cream if desired.

A Conversation with the Cook... "With the arrival of spring comes rhubarb with its tart, ruby-red stalks just waiting to be cooked into a special dessert. Just make sure you have plenty of sugar on hand to sweeten up this mouth-puckering plant."

Rhubarb Crunch

Makes 12 servings

Crumb Topping:
1 cup flour
1 cup brown sugar, packed
1 teaspoon cinnamon
3/4 cup uncooked rolled oats
1/2 cup melted butter

Fruit Mixture:
4 cups diced rhubarb
2 tablespoons corn starch
1 teaspoon vanilla
1 cup sugar, or more to taste (rhubarb can be very tart)
1 cup water

Mix together crumb topping and press 1/2 crumbs in 13 x 9-inch pan. Cover with the diced rhubarb. In small sauce pan combine sugar, cornstarch, water, and vanilla; cook stirring till thick and clear; pour over rhubarb. Top with remaining 1/2 crumbs. Bake 1 hour at 350°; when cooled put in refrigerator.

A Conversation with the Cook... "Can top with Cool Whip®, vanilla ice cream, or just pour on half-and-half cream."

Angel's 3-Layer Lemon Cake
Makes 12 servings

Batter for 3 (9-inch) Layers:
6 tablespoons butter
2 cups sugar
2 cups flour
1/4 teaspoon salt
3 teaspoons baking powder
6 egg yolks, well beaten
6 egg whites, beaten stiff
1 teaspoon lemon extract
7 tablespoons milk

Mix and sift flour, salt, and baking powder; set aside. Cream butter and sugar thoroughly. Add the well beaten egg yolks; then the flour mixture, the milk, and the lemon juice. Fold in stiffly beaten egg whites to make a light batter. Pour into 3 round 9-inch (greased and floured) pans and bake at 350° for 25 minutes. When cool spread the following filling between layers:

Lemon Filling:
1 1/2 cups sugar
1/2 cup butter
3 eggs
Juice and the grated rind (zest) of 2 lemons

Cream butter, sugar, and eggs together. Set into a dish of boiling water until heated; then add lemon, and bring to boil to thicken. Remove from heat and cool.

When cool, spread between layers of cake. For the final touch make following recipe for frosting:

Lemon Glaze Frosting
1/3 cup butter, softened
3 cups powdered sugar
1 tablespoon finely grated lemon zest (rind)
2 to 3 tablespoons lemon juice

A Conversation with the Cook... "Now, 'put the icing on the cake.'"

✧

Rice Krispies® Cookies
Makes about 6 1/2 dozen cookies

1 cup white sugar
1 cup brown sugar, packed
2 sticks butter, at room temperature
1 egg
1 teaspoon vanilla
1 cup olive oil
3 1/2 cups flour
1 teaspoon salt
1 teaspoon baking soda
1 teaspoon cream of tartar
1 cup Rice Krispies®
1 cup oatmeal
1/2 cup nuts, chopped
Sugar, at time of forming cookies

Cream butter, brown sugar, and white sugar. Add egg and vanilla. Mix well. Add oil and mix well again. Add flour, salt, baking soda, and cream of tartar; mix thouroughly. Add Rice Krispies®, oatmeal, and chopped nuts. Mix well with large spoon. Make into balls and place on cookie sheets. Flatten balls with bottom of glass dipped in sugar. Re-dip glass in sugar after each cookie is pressed. Bake at 350° for 10 minutes.

A Conversation with the Cook... "Be sure to only dip bottom of glass once in sugar for each pressing of a cookie, otherwise the cookies will have sugar caked on top after being baked. The sugar is basically to prevent the glass from sticking to the cookie dough as you press it into shape."

> *"C is for cookie, it's good enough for me;*
> *oh cookie, cookie, cookie starts with a C."*
> *~Cookie Monster, Sesame Street*

Coconut-Oatmeal Cookies

Makes about 3 1/2 dozen cookies

1 1/4 cups sifted flour
1 teaspoon baking powder
1 teaspoon baking soda
1/2 teaspoon salt
1/2 cup shortening
1/2 cup brown sugar, packed
1/2 cup white sugar
2 eggs
1 teaspoon vanilla
1 tablespoon milk
1 cup flaked coconut
1 cup quick cooking oats

Sift together flour, baking powder, baking soda, and salt; set aside. Using an electric mixer at medium speed, cream together shortening, brown sugar, and white sugar in bowl until light and fluffy. Add eggs, one at a time; beating well after each addition. Blend in vanilla and milk. Gradually add dry ingredients into creamed mixture, blending well. Stir in coconut and oats. Drop mixture by rounded-teaspoonfuls on greased baking sheets. Bake at 350° for 10 to 12 minutes.

A Conversation with the Cook... "When you come across the term 'shortening' in a recipe, it can mean a vegetable shortening (such as solid Crisco®), lard, butter, margarine, oleo, a mixture there of, or any solid fat used for baking."

Banana Chip Bars
Makes 16 bars

3/4 cup butter
2/3 cup granulated sugar
2/3 cup brown sugar, packed
1 egg
1 teaspoon vanilla
1 cup very ripe banana, peeled and mashed
2 cups flour
2 teaspoons baking powder
1/2 teaspoon salt
1 cup semi-sweet chocolate chips

Cream butter, brown sugar, and granulated sugar till fluffy. Add egg and vanilla, beat well. Stir in mashed banana. Stir together flour, baking powder, and salt. Add to creamed mixture; beat well. Fold in chocolate chips. Spread in greased and floured 13 x 9-inch baking pan. Bake at 375° for 35 to 40 minutes. Cool; cut into bars.

A Conversation with the Cook... "Don't throw out those bananas! Over-ripe bananas can be peeled and frozen in a plastic container until it's time to bake bread, cake, or bars."

Dottie's Danish Sugar Cookies
Makes 4 dozen

2 cups sifted all-purpose flour
3/4 teaspoon baking soda
1 teaspoon cream of tartar
1/4 teaspoon salt
1 cup powdered sugar
1/2 cup firm butter
1/2 cup vegetable shortening (such as Crisco®)
1 egg
1 teaspoon vanilla
Granulated sugar

Sift flour, baking soda, cream of tartar, salt, and powdered sugar into large bowl. Add butter and vegetable shortening. Mix at a low speed until mixture resembles coarse crumbs. Blend egg and vanilla. Add to dry ingredients. Mix only until blended. Dough is fairly soft. Shape into 1-inch balls. Roll balls in granulated sugar. Place 2 inches apart on un-greased cookie sheet. Flatten to 1/4-inch with bottom of glass dipped in granulated sugar. Bake at 350° for about 10 minutes or until edges get brown.

A Conversation with the Cook... "These cookies will melt in your mouth and you'll beg for more. In fact, these cookies will probably disappear faster than you can bake them!"

Trick or Treat Monster Cookies

"Mmmmmm—coooookiiiies"—flexible recipe: makes the equivalent of 6 dozen "normal" cookies

2 cups brown sugar, packed
2 cups white sugar
1 cup butter
9 cups quick oatmeal
1 1/2 teaspoons vanilla
6 eggs, beaten
4 teaspoons baking soda
3 cups peanut butter
1/2 pound chocolate chips
1/2 pound M&M® candy

Cream butter and sugar. Add beaten eggs and remaining ingredients. Fill an ice cream scoop and drop on cookie sheet. Flatten a little with your hand. Do not put too close together as they get "very large." It is best to bake one so you can see. Bake at 350° for 8 to 10 minutes. Do not over bake.

A Conversation with the Cook... "To make as bars, use a jelly roll pan, and spread out dough in thin layer to fill pan. Bars may have to stay in the oven a few minutes more, as the tray of dough will take longer to bake. Or, bake as one truly 'Monster Cookie' in a round pizza pan! Cut wedges with a pizza cutter and serve."

Mother's Almond Crescents

Makes 3 dozen cookies

1 cup butter
2 tablespoons powdered sugar
2 cups flour
1 teaspoon vanilla
1/2 teaspoon salt
1/4 pound blanched almonds, grated
Additional powdered sugar

Mix together all ingredients (except additional powdered sugar); chill dough. Roll out and form into small crescent shapes. Place on cookie sheet and bake at 350° for 10 to 15 minutes. Roll in powdered sugar while still warm. Cookies will be very tender.

A Conversation with the Cook... "My Mother made these every Christmas. I don't know who ate more of them my Dad or me."

"Laughter is brightest, in the place where food is."
~Irish Proverb

Gingerbread-Currant Cakes-in-a-Jar
Novelty recipe, great for gift-giving

3/4 cup currants
3 cups flour, divided
2 teaspoons baking soda
1 cup buttermilk (or can use sour milk, see page 264)
1 cup molasses
1 1/2 teaspoons ginger
1 teaspoon cinnamon
1/2 cup butter, slightly softened
1 cup sugar
1 egg
6 (1-pint) wide-mouthed, straight-sided Mason® or Kerr® glass jars with appropriate lids (you will need 8 jars for larger recipes, like commercial cake mixes—your recipe does not have to be homemade-from-scratch!)

Roll currants to coat in 1/2 cup flour; set aside. Mix baking soda, buttermilk and molasses; set aside. Sift together remaining 2 1/2 cups flour, ginger, cinnamon; set aside. Cream butter and sugar together; blend in egg. Add in molasses mixture and flour mixture, alternately, blending each addition. Lastly fold in currants. Generously grease insides of each sterilized (see page 232) jar with shortening. Carefully pour 1 cup batter into each jar—jars should be filled half-way. (Cake will rise as it bakes.) Wipe off any spills on rims with a paper towel. Set jars on a cookie sheet and bake in a 325° degree oven, until tooth-pick-test in center comes out clean—about 40 minutes. Remove jars one-at-a-time from oven and immediately screw on a sterilized lid to create a vacuum seal. Make sure rim of jar is still clean (again wiping with paper towel if needed) so you get a proper seal. Let jars cool on the kitchen counter. You will hear the lids "ping" as they indent to form their proper seal. Store sealed cakes in fridge for up to 2 weeks, or longer in the freezer. Pop one out when you want a snack!

A Conversation with the Cook... "Just for fun, make a cake for each dinner guest, decorate the jars, put on a name tag, and use at table settings as a 'place card.' If your guests are too full for dessert after dinner, they can take it home!"

> *"Travel light in life, take only what you need:*
> *a loving family, good friends, simple pleasures,*
> *someone to love, and someone to love you,*
> *enough to eat, enough to wear, and a little more than*
> *enough to drink..."*
> *~unknown*

A Special Thank You ...

to all of our friends and relatives, mothers and grandmothers, daughters and sons, and husbands too—who have provided many-a-recipe for this book:

Audra Le Normand, Liberty Texas

Judy Brown, Midland Michigan

The Rush Hour Cook, Brook Noel,
Milwaukee Wisconsin

Angie, Sara, Donna, Carla, June, Suzi, Nancy, and Sammy

Glenn, Caleb, Andy, and Karl

—in our house there are never too many cooks in the kitchen!

Wendy Louise and MaryAnn

Recipe Index

Appetizers and Snacks
Almond, Toasted Party Spread, 43
Avocado Puffs, 17
Bacon Bites, Bernie's, 31
Bacon Tomato Cups, 25
Bacon Wrapped Bread Sticks, 24
Bean Dip, 30
Chicken Puffs, 38
Chicken Wings, Oh So Good, 35
Crab Quiche with Savory Crumb
    Crust, Marilyn's, 18
Easy Italian Pinwheels, 29
Florida Crackers, 19
Granola Grande, 32
Natural Munch, 31
Olive Shortbread Cookies, 33
Party Pecans, Pearlie Mae's, 20
Pizza, Lite Vegetable, 26
Potato Nachos, MAK'S, 34
Prize Potato Chips, 21
Ranch Oyster Crackers Snack, 33
Sausage Bites, 27
Seafood Puffs, 37
Spinach-Cheese Squares, 36
Spinach Dip, Sara's Sassy, 32
Stacker Crackers, Sammy's, 22
Stuffed Mushrooms, 28
Sugar Baked Peanuts, 20
Tomato Pesto Pie, 23

Bacon
Bacon Bites, Bernie's, 31
Bacon Tomato Cups, 25
Bacon Wrapped Bread Sticks, 24

Karl's "Kuiche," 79
Liver Spanish Style, 59
MaryAnn's Versatile Southwest
　　Bean Bake, 194

Beans and Lentils
Bean Dip, 30
MaryAnn's Versatile Southwest
　　Bean Bake, 194

Beef
Angel's Beef and Potato Bake, 184
Baked Chop Suey, Alicia's, 62
Baked Tenderloin, Grandma Scherer's, 150
Beef Noodle Casserole, 183
Beef Pastie Pie, Mrs. Dalle Ave's, 81
Beef "Summer Sausage," Helga's
　　Homemade, 86
Braised Rib-Eye Steaks, 158
Casserole Beef Stew, 170
Clay Pot Meat Loaf, Dorothea's, 76
Easy and Good Beef and Biscuits, 187
Family Favorite Beef Taco Bake, 53
Hunter's Delight, 58
Impossible Taco Pie, 66
Italian Beef, Angie's, 56
Italian Roast Dinner, 105
Liver Spanish Style, 59
Mediterranean Pot Roast, 141
My Garden Stuffed Zucchini Boats, 76
Oven Stew, 60
Oven Roasting Beef 101, 131
Pepper Steak, MaryAnn's, 102
Pizza Pop-Up Casserole, 183
Roast Rib-Eye, Mary's, 157
Round Steak and Ravioli, 180
Sicilian Meat Loaf, Grandma's, 87
Stuffed Green Peppers, 89

Stuffed Tomatoes, 89
Super Supper Roast, Angie's, 61
Too Easy Pot Roast, 49
Taco Casserole, 106

Beverages
Café Delmonico Dessert Coffee, 237
Donna's Homemade Baileys
    Cream After-Dinner Drink, 236
Sun Tea, 238

Breads
All Season Bread, Bobbie's, 262
Aunt Emma's Hot Corn Bread, 267
Beer Bread, Caleb's, 269
Biscuits, I Slaved All Day
    Cheddar and Herb, 268
Biscuits, Old Fashioned Corn, 290
Biscuits, Sweet Potato, 285
Butterhorns, 277
Coffee Cake, Cereal, 293
Coffee Cake, Peach, 278
Coffeecake, Sour Cream, 287
Chocolate Banana Bread, 275
Cinnamon Zucchini Bread, 276
Corn Bread, 266
Date Nut Bread, 261
French Bread, Sara's No-Fail, 257
Fresh Pretzels, 288
Irish Oatmeal Bread, 292
Lemon Bread, 260
Liz's Soft-Baked Bread Sticks, 272
Mushroom Stuffed Crescent Rolls, 259
Popovers, Auntie Joan's, 271
Pumpkin Bread, Angie's, 274
Rhubarb Nut Bread, 264

Cakes and Icings
Angel's 3-Layer Lemon Cake, 333
 -Lemon Glaze Frosting for, 333
Buttersctotch Cake, 324
 -Glaze for, 324
Chocolate Chocolate-Chip
 Zucchini Cake, 319
Fruit Cocktail Cake, 327
Gingerbread-Currant
 Cakes-in-a-Jar, 341
Honey Cake, 321
 -Frosting for, 321
Poppy Seed Pound Cake, 315
Rich Devil's Food Cake, 323
 -Simple Vanilla Frosting for, 323
 -Browned Butter Frosting for, 323
Sour Cream Cake, 313
Strawberry Cake, 328

Cheese
Cazuela de Quesa y Championes
 (Casserole of Baked Cheese and
 Mushrooms), 163
Cheese Strata with Corn Flake
 Topping, 43

Chicken
Budin Chicken Tortilla Bake, 117
Cashew Chicken, Suzanne's, 103
Chicken Bake No Peek, 152
Chicken Breasts with Cheese
 and Tomato, 55
Chicken Cacciatore, Breanne's, 104
Chicken and Rice Casserole, Audra's, 45
Chicken Enchiladas, 64
Chicken in a Clay Pot, 114
Chicken Pot Pie, Glenn's Old-
 Fashioned Taste, 92

Chicken Puffs, 38
Chicken Royale, Mom's, 122
Chicken Tetrazzini, MaryAnn's, 94
Chicken Wings, Oh So Good, 35
Countryside Chicken Bake, 93
Divine Chicken Divan, 119
   Bonus-Recipe: Chicken Broccoli
   Crepes, 121
Enchiladas Acapulco, 124
Hot Chicken Salad, Angie's, 185
New Orleans-Style Chicken, 153
Peach-Stuffed Chicken Breasts, 142
Poppy Seed Chicken, 67
The King's Chicken, 44
Yorkshire Chicken Bake, 111
Wild Rice Chicken Bake, 112

Condiments, Relishes, Dips, and Garnishes
Applesauce, Lucile's Homemade, 215
Baked Hot Fruit Compote, 207
Betty's 25 Tomato Catsup, 242
Change-of-Pace Salsa, 220
Corn Salsa, 222
Cranberry Chutney, 228
Crème Fraiche, 217
Frozen Cranberry-Cream Mold, 227
Mayonnaise Frenchaise, 216
New Mexican Salsa Cruda, 221
Rose Wine Jelly, 231
Smooth Avocado Sauce, 216
Tartar Sauce, MaryAnn's, 218
Thousand Island Dressing, Dip
   or Condiment, 218

Cookies
Banana Chip Bars, 337
Chocolate Mint Brownies, 317
Coconut-Oatmeal Cookies, 336

Dottie's Danish Sugar Cookies, 338
Mother's Almond Crescents, 340
Rice Krispies® Cookies, 334
Trick or Treat Monster Cookies, 339

Desserts
Creamy Apple Dessert, 320
Mother's Old Fashioned
    Bread Pudding, 312
"Next Day" Meringue Shells, 316
Noodle-Kugel Pudding, June's, 206
Pear & Cranberry Upside Down
    Cake, 309
Pineapple Upside Down Cake,
    Margarite's, 307
Plum Cake, Peggy's, 310
Rhubarb Crunch, 332
Rhubarb Special, 330

Fish and Seafood
Crab Carib, Auntie Joan's, 126
Crab Quiche with Savory Crumb
    Crust, Marilyn's, 18
Golden Fish Puffs, MaryAnn's, 54
Red Snapper with Garden Sauce, 144
Salmon Casserole, Glenn's, 68
Seafood Hot Dish, Angie's, 186
Seafood Medley, 166
Seafood N Biscuits Cobbler, 168
Seafood Puffs, 37
Shrimp d'Jonghe, 171
Tuna Casserole, Annabelle's, 172

Fruit Dishes
Applesauce, Lucile's Homemade, 215
Baked Hot Fruit Compote, 207
Cranberry Chutney, 228
Fresh Fruit Tray

with "Frosted" Grapes, 225
Frozen Cranberry-Cream Mold, 227
Glazed Carrots with Red Grapes,
     Marilyn's, 240
Liz's Lemon Curd, 229

Gravies and Sauces
Fresh Peach Sauce, 142
Madeira Sauce (for roasted meats), 132
Turkey Pan Gravy, 133

Ham
Baked Glazed Ham, Mom's, 84
Ham and Broccoli Roll-Ups, 48

Lamb
Sunday Roast Leg of Lamb, with Oven
     Roasted Potatoes and Gravy, 71

Miscellaneous
Big Apple Pancake, 291
Betty's 25 Tomato Catsup, 242
Donald's "Dogs," 85
Fresh Pretzels, 288
Helga's Homemade Beef
     "Summer Sausage," 86
Gingerbread-Currant
     Cakes-in-a-Jar, 341
Puff Pastry, 36, 37, 306

Molded Salads
Asparagus Molded Salad, 253
Frozen Cranberry-Cream Mold, 227
Marshmallow Mint Salad, 246
Orange Sherbet Gelatin Salad, 250
Sunny Summery Gelatin Mold, 223
Surprise Gelatin Salad, 247
Terrific Tomato Aspic, 224

Muffins
Banana Chocolate-Chip Muffins, 280
Carrot and Pineapple Muffins, 286
Cinnamon Muffins, 270
Dottie's Blueberry Muffins, 281

Noodles and Pasta
Baked Stuffed Shells, Grandma Scherer's, 177
Beef Noodle Casserole, 183
Chicken Tetrazzini, MaryAnn's, 94
Easy Everyday Lasagna, 99
Great Spaghetti Bake, 175
Macaroni Salad, 252
Manicotti, Grandma Scherer's Side-by-Side, 100
Noodle-Kugel Pudding, June's, 206
Pizza Noodle Hot Dish, Glenn's, 52
Round Steak and Ravioli, 180
Salmon Casserole, Glenn's, 68
Scalloped Apple Noodle Bake, MAK and LOUISE, 80
Tuna Casserole, Annabelle's, 172
Vegetarian Lasagna, 96
Wieneroni Casserole, Sammy's, 173

Pies
Pie Crust, Aunt Louise's Formula for, 297
Chocolate Pie Divine, Gail's, 302
Cranberry Apple Pie, 299
Easy and Elegant Summer Fruit Pie, 301
Pineapple Cheese Pie, Lucile's, 305
Pineapple Cream Pie, Linda's, 305
Prune Pie, Peggy's, 304
Puff Pastry, for Cream Puffs, 306
Southern Chess Pie, 303
Summer Peach Parfait Pie, 300

Pork
BBQ Baby Back Ribs, Dad's, 51
Clay Pot Pork Roast, 116
Glazed Pork Tenderloin, Suzanne's, 151
Hawaiian Spareribs, 156
Oven Baked Pork, Glenn's, 57
Pork Casserole, 188
Pork Chop Casserole, Mom's, 47
Pork Chops with Tomato-
    Olive Sauce, 149
Stuffed Crown Roast of Pork, 147
Stuffed Pork Chops, Glenn's, 155

Potatoes
Angel's Beef and Potato Bake, 184
Baked Hash Brown Side
    Dish, Shirley's, 191
Double-Baked Potatoes Parmesan, 193
German Potato Salad for a Crowd, 245
Mother's Scalloped Potatoes, 192
Potato Broccoli Bake, Audra's, 210
Potato Nachos, MAK'S, 34
Potato Pie, Peggy's, 50

Rice
Chicken and Rice Casserole, Audra's, 45
Stuffed Tomatoes, 89
Suzi's Mexican Vegetarian Casserole, 165
Wild Rice Chicken Bake, 112
(Never Fail) Wild Rice Side Dish, 145

Salad
Creamed Onions, 251
Dieter's Delight, 248
German Potato Salad for a Crowd, 245
Macaroni Salad, 252
MaryAnn's Bean Salad or Relish, 241
Raspberry Vinaigrette Salad, Carla's, 235

Steven's Country Salad, 249
Tomato and Cumber Salad, 244

Sausage
Helga's Homemade Beef
 "Summer Sausage," 86
Old Fashioned Sausages and
 Sauerkraut, 91
Sausage Bites, 27

Sauces (see Gravies)
Seafood (see Fish)
Snacks (see Appetizers)

Stuffing
Stuffing-on-the-Side, 133

Turkey and Fowl
Roast Cornish Hens, 145
Traditional Roast Turkey with Pan Gravy
 and Stuffing-on-the-Side, 133
Turkey Loaf, MaryAnn's Magic, 63

Veal
Classic French Farmhouse Veal Roast, 73
Venetian Veal Pie, Barbara's, 128

Vegetables
Artichoke Heart Casserole, 201
Asparagus au Parmesan, Mom's, 197
Asparagus Quiche Lorraine, 98
Baked Carrot Mold, June's, 204
Betty's Celery Bake Side-Dish, 200
Brown Sugar Tomato Bake, 211
Copper Carrot Pennies, 239
Corn Pudding, 196
Creamy Cheddar Corn and Broccoli, 254
Dorothy's Cabbage Casserole, 199

Garden Supper Dish. Suzanne's, 174
Glazed Carrots with Red
    Grapes, Marilyn's, 240
Grilled Garden Tomatoes, Mother's, 234
Madame's Yams, 203
Mediterranean Zucchini Bake, 169
My Garden Stuffed Zucchini Boats, 76
Mushroom Pie, 78
Old Fashioned Sausages
    and Sauerkraut, 91
Potato Broccoli Bake, Audra's, 210
Spinach-Cheese Squares, 36
Spinach Dip, Sara's Sassy, 32
Spinach Quiche Pie, 202
Stuffed Green Peppers, 89
Stuffed Mushrooms, 28
Stuffed Tomatoes, 89
Tomato Pesto Pie, 23

(Some) Vegetarian Suggestions
Baked Stuffed Shells, Grandma
    Scherer's, 177
Brown Sugar Tomato Bake, 211
Corn Pudding, 196
Creamy Cheddar Corn and Broccoli, 254
Dorothy's Cabbage Casserole, 199
Great Spaghetti Bake, 175
Grilled Garden Tomatoes, Mother's, 234
Koopman's Favorite Baked Dish, 209
Potato Broccoli Bake, Audra's, 210
Suzi's Mexican Vegetarian Casserole, 165
Vegetarian Lasagna, 96